ULTRA HIGH QUALITY

FILMLANDIA!

PNW

☐ SP.   ☐ LP   ☐ EP

D0052238

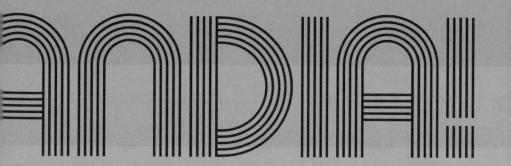

A Movie Lover's Guide to the Films and Television of Seattle, Portland, and the Great Northwest

DAVID SCHMADER

Illustrated by Ashod Simonian

SASQUATCH BOOKS
SEATTLE

Printed in China

SASQUATCH BOOKS with colophon is a registered trademark of Penguin Random House LLC

27 26 25 24 23   9 8 7 6 5 4 3 2 1

Illustrator: Ashod Simonian
Editor: Jen Worick
Production editor: Peggy Gannon
Designer: Tony Ong

Library of Congress Cataloging-in-Publication Data

Names: Schmader, David, author.
Title: Filmlandia! : a movie-lover's guide to the films and television of
   Seattle, Portland, and the Great Northwest / David Schmader ;
   illustrated by Ashod Simonian.
Description: Seattle : Sasquatch Books, [2023] | Includes index.
Identifiers: LCCN 2022028268 (print) | LCCN 2022028269 (ebook) | ISBN
   9781632174253 (paperback) | ISBN 9781632174260 (epub)
Subjects: LCSH: Motion picture locations--Washington (State)--Guidebooks. |
   Motion picture locations--Oregon--Guidebooks. | Motion picture
   locations--Northwest, Pacific--Guidebooks.
Classification: LCC PN1995.67.W375 A44 2005 (print) | LCC PN1995.67.W375
   (ebook) | DDC 791.4302/509797--dc23/eng/20220902
LC record available at https://lccn.loc.gov/2022028268
LC ebook record available at https://lccn.loc.gov/2022028269

ISBN: 978-1-63217-425-3

Sasquatch Books
1325 Fourth Avenue, Suite 1025
Seattle, WA 98101

SasquatchBooks.com

This book is dedicated to my mom, who never stopped supporting and sharing my love for movies, from the day she allowed 11-year-old me to skip school so we could attend a matinee of the re-released *The Sound of Music*, to the week in the early aughts when she flew to Seattle to see Matthew Barney's *Cremaster Cycle* with me at the Varsity Cinema, to that weird Sunday night in 1985 when neither of us could sleep so we met up in the living room at 2 a.m. to watch a late-night screening of *The Rose*.

CONTENTS

Introduction
A Film Lover's Paradise

For filmmakers, the Pacific Northwest presents a double whammy of ravishing cinematic locales, offering hypermodern cityscapes amid vast natural splendor. Here moviemakers find a reliable setting for all sorts of cloudy human experiences: with perpetual sogginess, low skies, and sporadic blasts of sun forming a pressure cooker for drama—from love-starved vampires and obsessive con artists to poetic junkies and the nation's most vengeful divorcées.

But alongside the mossy noirs have bloomed some of the most romantic love stories that still manage to feel like real life, and the whole region has served to cultivate and inspire such world-class cinematic talents as Gus Van Sant, Kelly Reichardt, and Lynn Shelton. Beyond this are the non-cinema visual entertainments—the Frasiers, Portlandias, and Grey's Anatomies, all drawing on the unique cultural character of the Pacific Northwest.

During initial planning of this book, I assumed I'd be dealing with eighty to ninety films. But as I worked through those, more and more titles started to trickle in, and in the end I watched over two hundred. Still, this book is not exhaustive, just alphabetical, with entries split between Washington (where the primary visual motif is a glistening cityscape before a snow-capped mountain; bonus points for Space Needles) and Oregon (where the primary visual motifs are trees and bridges, bridges, bridges).

SEATTLE &
WASHINGTON

"Everywhere you look there's something to film." So said *Streetwise* and *American Heart* director Martin Bell about the cinematic attractiveness of Seattle. This sentiment is echoed by Jennifer Lopez's overexcited daughter in the revenge thriller *Enough*. Entering Seattle from the south via the viaduct, in a convertible while overlooking Puget Sound on the sunniest day of the year, she exclaims, "Wow! This city really sparkles!"

That kid is not wrong. *New York Times* critic Stephen Holden took it further, describing Seattle in his 1997 review of *Slaves to the Underground* as "America's dreamiest big city."

But don't just listen to the critics and child actors. Listen to *me*. The following pages are a guided tour of Seattle-centric cinema from blockbusters to indies, sorting the work of serious Seattle channelers from that of mere location-users. (Telltale signs of underinformed interlopers: depicting Seattle rain as a pummeling downpour rather than perpetual drizzle, pronouncing the University of Washington's abbreviated moniker "UW" as "You Double-U" instead of the proper "U-Dub.") As mentioned, the following list of Seattle films is not exhaustive, just alphabetical. (And documentaries are grouped together on page 86.) Roll 'em!

10 THINGS I HATE ABOUT YOU

(1999, DIR. GIL JUNGER)

From the opening shot of Seattle being scribbled into existence to the final aerial view of Letters to Cleo performing atop Tacoma's Stadium High School, this late-nineties spin on *The Taming of the Shrew* is a crucial entry in the PNW cinema canon. It's also one of the most beloved teen rom-coms of its generation, introducing Heath Ledger as a uniquely charismatic screen presence (with star-enhancing support from co-star Joseph Gordon-Levitt) and finding a fittingly Northwesty heroine in Julia Stiles's Kat, a devoted feminist buzzkill with a heart of gold.

continued...

As for local attractions, our romantic lead's crucial day-date takes place in the Seattle neighborhood of Fremont, where the duo beholds the Fremont Troll statue, paddles a boat on Lake Union, and shares a first kiss in a pile of hay at Gasworks Park. The climactic Padua Prom makes use of two Seattle landmarks: downtown's Paramount Theatre (home of the prom's lavish lobby) and Capitol Hill's Century Ballroom, home to the prom itself. Finally, there's Padua High School—which is "portrayed" by Tacoma's historic and movie-star gorgeous Stadium High School and adjacent Stadium Bowl, a fifteen thousand–seat stadium with stunning views of Puget Sound.

21 & OVER
(2013, DIRS. JON LUCAS AND SCOTT MOORE)

From the creators of the *Hangover* trilogy comes this night-on-the-town shock comedy in which a trio of repellent college students (played by Miles Teller, Skylar Astin, and Justin Chon) celebrate a twenty-first birthday and instigate a madcap night of public urination, penis torture, and slow-motion barf on a mechanical bull. They also visit the University District bars Finn MacCools and Big Time Brewery, ramble around frat houses on a makeshift Greek Row situated on Capitol Hill's Federal Avenue, and wind up at a music festival at the Gorge Amphitheater.

50 SHADES OF GREY
(2015, DIR. SAM TAYLOR-JOHNSON)

Based on the *Twilight* fanfic turned bestselling novel, the cinematic adaptation of E L James's blockbuster BDSM bodice-ripper stars Dakota Johnson as a virginal waif drawn into the kinky world of a suit-wearing man played by Jamie Dornan (in a suit). Despite being filmed almost entirely in British Columbia,

50 Shades exerts itself to feel like a Seattle movie, showcasing a dazzling nighttime helicopter ride over downtown and practically fetishizing the city's damp, overcast vibe. Also, Mr. Grey's tricked-out penthouse (the exterior at least) is located at the top of the Escala tower in Seattle's Belltown neighborhood. In 2013, the actual penthouse sold for $6.2 million.

99 AND 44/100% DEAD
(1974, DIR. JOHN FRANKENHEIMER)

Hitting the screen with a pop-art credit sequence created by Roy Lichtenstein, this satirical crime thriller tracks the blood-soaked turf war between two factions of the mob and their respective hit men on the streets of downtown Seattle. Originally to be directed by Sergio Leone with Marcello Mastroianni and Charles Bronson in the leads, the film eventually passed to John Frankenheimer

continued . . .

and stars Richard Harris and Edmond O'Brien. The result is a grimy crime caper with a *Reservoir-Dogs*-meets-*Blues-Brothers* feel, miles of explosive car chases, and some seriously twisted sex stuff. (When a sadistic man with a hook hand meets a compliant white-collar prostitute, everyone loses.) It's all proudly and satirically crass as shit, with exploding vehicles being riddled with bullets as they plunge into Puget Sound and plot points involving Miami alligators in Seattle sewers. It also makes dramatic use of Seattle, from a Pike Place Market shootout to an inflatable art exhibit at Seattle Art Museum to the film's most poetic shot: a slew of concrete shoes anchored to the floor of Puget Sound, many with their mob-displeasing humans still floating above them, creating an underwater garden of people done wrong.

AMERICAN HEART
(1992, DIR. MARTIN BELL)

From the director of the classic Seattle documentary *Streetwise* comes this fictionalized exploration of the Seattle street scene. Jeff Bridges and Edward Furlong star as an ex-con father and his adolescent son rebuilding their lives and reestablishing their connection on Seattle's hardscrabble downtown streets. It's a poetically grim affair, filmed with a restricted color palette of yellow and brown and featuring life-sized, proto-mumblecore performances. Bridges cites the role as his career favorite, but it's awkward hatchling Furlong, with his pubescent androgyny and literal suitcase of memories, who gives the film its soul, capturing the cumulative strength and vulnerability of the source documentary's original kids. Besides being a grim, beige docudrama, *American Heart* is an ace time capsule of early-nineties Seattle, replete with shots of dive bars filled with people smoking, Sisters of Perpetual Indulgence roaming the street, and a relatively undeveloped downtown core.

THE ART OF RACING IN THE RAIN

(2019, DIR. SIMON CURTIS)

Based on the bestselling novel by
Seattle author Garth Stein, *The
Art of Racing in the Rain* concerns
an aspiring professional race-car
driver and his spiritual-mystic dog,
the latter of which thinks in the
voice of Kevin Costner and finds
profound life lessons in his master's
career. Eventually the man (played
by Milo Ventimiglia) meets a woman (Amanda Seyfried), ushering in
a world of family drama and medical strife, guaranteeing to jerk your
tears. As for locales, nearly everything was shot in Canada, with some
California and Italy thrown in, but there's a nice establishing shot
of King County Superior Court, and Kent's Pacific Raceways is our
human hero's home racetrack.

ASSASSINS

(1995, DIR. RICHARD DONNER)

Sylvester Stallone stars as a hitman hungry to retire, Antonio
Banderas co-stars as a rival hitman who only wants to fatally shoot
Stallone before he retires, and Julianne Moore provides support
as a computer hacker who helps Sly best Banderas, and oh my
God it's all dumb and boring with random explosions and
inexplicable action and a script so bad the original writers (the
Wachowskis!) tried to have their names removed. Still, this boring
mess was shot almost entirely in the beautiful Puget Sound region
and features such notable sights as the Monorail, the Aurora Bridge,
Evergreen Cemetery in North Seattle, and too many rain-slicked
streets to count.

DYSTOPIAN FUTURES

As a setting for future shock and post-apocalyptic ruin, the Pacific Northwest has proven uniquely attractive to filmmakers. The (dis)honor roll:

THE ROAD (2009, DIR. JOHN HILLCOAT) Cormac McCarthy's brutally bleak, redemptively brilliant novel *The Road* tracks a father and son's daily fight for survival in a mid-apocalyptic wasteland. For the brutally bleak, sporadically brilliant cinema adaptation starring Viggo Mortensen and Kodi Smit-McPhee, the production team surveyed terrain hit by natural and manmade disasters, then "chose the bleakest places and filmed them," as director John Hillcoat says in a making-of featurette. Among these bleakest of places: Mount Saint Helens, the active volcano located in Skamania County, Washington, whose 1980 eruption killed 57 people, left an otherworldly mile-wide crater, and where "the world of the book came alive!" says Hillcoat.

THE POSTMAN (1997, DIR. KEVIN COSTNER) In the faraway future of 2013, an unnamed man wanders post-apocalyptic America in a postman's uniform, delivering mail and filling dusty townsfolk with hope. This is the plot of Kevin Costner's *The Postman*, the dull, overlong, and hilariously self-serious film that earned Costner Worst Actor, Worst Director, and Worst Picture at the 1998 Razzies. Still, there are interesting supporting players (Olivia Williams from *Rushmore*, Tom Petty from The Heartbreakers) and some good PNW locales, including the area around Metaline Falls, Washington (which provided both the fictional Bridge City and the fictional Pineview community), and Anacortes, Washington, where the movie reaches its blessed end.

CLASS OF 1999 (1990, DIR. MARK L. LESTER) Made in 1990 and set nine years later, this rollickingly trashy flick concerns a Seattle high school so overrun with violent crime that human teachers are replaced with repurposed military cyborgs, one of whom looks exactly like Pam Grier and who's not above stabbing recalcitrant students with her high heels. Clearly, it's awesome, with the fictional Kennedy High School set at Seattle's Lincoln High School and a crucial scene in which the killer robot teachers emerge spookily from the waters of Puget Sound.

BATTLE IN SEATTLE

(2007, DIR. STUART TOWNSEND)

A docudrama about an event a generation of Seattleites will always remember, *Battle in Seattle* concerns the city's hosting of the World Trade Organization's Ministerial Conference of 1999 and the tens of thousands of demonstrators who took to the streets to shut this worker- and environment-exploiting nonsense down. Starring André 3000 as a protester in a walkabout sea turtle costume and Ray Liotta as a mayor in a wig, the movie throws viewers into the thick of the protest's planning and execution, kicking off with a nerve-racking dangling-from-a-crane sequence, climaxing with a harrowing street fight that put Charlize Theron in the hospital, and featuring many dramatic shots of tear-gassed eyes being rinsed. Despite the credible you-are-there vibe, we are not actually there—most of the film was shot in Vancouver with a few crucial scenes (the showdown outside Paramount Theatre, the rally at Key Arena, the march past Cinerama) set in the titular city.

BEACON HILL BOYS

(1985, DIRS. KEN MOCHIZUKI AND DEAN HAYASAKA)

Based on co-director Ken Mochizuki's novel about young Japanese American men navigating early seventies life in Seattle's Beacon Hill neighborhood, this beloved independent production was the first feature film ever made about Asian American youth. It was also a true community endeavor, with crucial support coming from the Northwest Asian American Theater, the *International Examiner* newspaper, and Seattle's Asian American and Pacific Islander community at large. Premiering to sold-out houses at the Nippon Kan Theatre in 1985, *Beacon Hill Boys* enjoyed a thirtieth anniversary screening at Seattle's Wing Luke Museum and is now seemingly impossible to view anywhere. Happy hunting!

BRUCE LEE

One of a handful of truly international superstars, Bruce Lee rocked
a career that straddled East and West. He had deep roots in Seattle,
where the San Francisco–born, Hong Kong–raised Lee moved in
1959, working as a waiter at Ruby Chow's, enrolling at the University
of Washington in 1961, and commencing teaching the martial arts
that would make him a cinema sensation the world over. Upon his
death in 1973, Bruce Lee returned to his wife's hometown of Seattle,
where he's buried (alongside his son, Brandon) at Capitol Hill's Lake
View Cemetery.

BENNY & JOON

(1993, DIR. JEREMIAH S. CHECHIK)

Joon (Mary Stuart Masterson) is a young woman with a disabling
mental illness who likes to don snorkeling gear to direct traffic with
ping-pong paddles and is also a large-scale abstract painter. Benny
(Aidan Quinn) is her caretaker brother, sacrificing his ambitions
to make sure Joon has a proper home in the world. (In this case,
the world is Spokane, Washington.) And Sam (Johnny Depp) is a
Buster Keaton impersonator whose illiteracy is cured by Benny's
reading lessons and whose heart is captured by Joon. Excepting
the opening train scenes shot near Metaline Falls, Washington, the
movie was shot on location in Spokane. Benny and Joon's house is
located in the Peaceful Valley neighborhood, and the café where
Ruthie (Julianne Moore) works and woos Benny is the famous
Mary Lou's Milk Bottle in the Garland District.

BIG IN JAPAN

(2014, DIR. JOHN JEFFCOAT)

Struggling to find an audience in their hometown, Seattle band Tennis Pro accepts an offer to take their act to—surprise!—Japan. Director John Jeffcoat follows this actual band improvising their way through a concocted scenario like a documentarian, as the members of Tennis Pro wander into an alternate existence where an American band has an inherent draw, and their old lives feel like a dream. The vast majority of the movie takes place in Tokyo, but the plot-engendering setup—a ghost town of a show that confirms Tennis Pro's creative isolation—goes down at the Seattle club The Showbox.

A BIT OF BAD LUCK

(2014, DIR. JOHN FUHRMAN)

Moviegoers fell in love with Cary Elwes for his dashing yet doofy romantic hero in *The Princess Bride*. It's unsure who will fall in love with Cary Elwes as the hero of *A Bit of Bad Luck*, in which he plays an unfaithful husband whose vengeful lumber-heiress wife subjects him to a parade of elaborate torments in rural Washington State. It's played like a kooky comedic morality tale, but it's . . . something else. I'll stand over here while the *Los Angeles Times* tells it like it is: "Cursed with obnoxiously broad characters and nonsensical plotting, *A Bit of Bad Luck* is an intended backwoods satire that runs hopelessly off-course from the outset." Filmed in Seattle and Morton, Washington!

GREY'S ANATOMY

(2005–PRESENT, ABC) As I write this, *Grey's Anatomy*—the high-drama, romance-packed medical series set at the fictional Seattle Grace Hospital—is broadcasting its eighteenth season, and there's no reason to believe it will ever end. (In 2021's Season 17, Dr. Meredith Grey survived Covid!) Conceived by budding TV titan Shonda Rhimes and roiling with hot doctors, freaky patients, and tear-jerking musical montages, *Grey's* delivers an entertainment nutrient that America apparently needs to survive. It also showcases a lot of Seattle, at least on the outside: the Space Needle–adjacent KOMO Plaza (with its rooftop helipad) supplies the exterior of the show's Seattle Grace Hospital, while some interiors are shot at a VA hospital in Los Angeles. The show's infamous Intern House is located on Queen Anne Hill, and the characters' favorite meeting place is view-packed Kerry Park—but most other scenes are shot at ABC TV studios in LA.

BLACK WIDOW
(1987, DIR. BOB RAFELSON)

Only one segment of this episodic, location-hopping investigative thriller takes place in the Pacific Northwest. But it is an incredible segment wherein our obsessed investigator (Debra Winger) tracks her murder-suspect prey (Theresa Russell) to Seattle, where the latter commences a new round of her patented marry-a-rich-man-then-kill-him routine. The blank-faced Russell is shown applying herself to the study of Coast Salish artifacts—so she can attract, seduce, and eventually bring about the death of the chairman of the Native American Museum Board. Posing as a reporter from the *Seattle Post-Intelligencer*, Debra Winger follows her around Seattle, which involves lots of car-ferry travel and perpetual front-of-ferry parking. After Seattle, the pair's chase takes them to Hawaii, where shit gets really twisty, and . . . you should just watch it. In a million other versions of this story, the role of the obsessed investigator would've been played by a male, and the tension would've been formulaic: "Is his obsession with the female criminal professional or sexual, and are they going to fall in love?" But making our obsessed hunter a huntress opens up a world of tension involving ambition, competition, jealousy, and sisterhood, on top of making the most of "Is this professional or sexual, and are they going to fall in love?"

THE BOOK OF STARS
(1999, DIR. MICHAEL MINER)

Something of a gritty, downbeat *Benny & Joon*, *The Book of Stars* features Jenna Malone as a young Seattle girl with cystic fibrosis and Mary Stuart Masterson as her devoted older sister who helps pay for her kid sister's medical treatment (and her own drugs) through sex work. Shining through the grimness is faith in the human spirit, represented through a perspective-enhancing neighbor, an artistic scrapbook, and the power of poetry. Directed by one of the writers of *RoboCop*!

BOY CULTURE
(2006, DIR. Q. ALLAN BROCKA)

Based on Matthew Rettenmund's 1995 novel, *Boy Culture* follows a snarky male escort in Seattle as he navigates twisty relationships with his roommates and a mysterious client. Steeped in conventional morality served up gay 'n' bitchy, the movie's a serious time capsule of gay Seattle with our hero traipsing through legendary landmarks, from the country-and-western gay bar the Timberline to Bailey/Coy Books on Broadway to the gorgeous and cruisy Volunteer Park. Bonus: the movie's characters pronounce the University of Washington's "UW" nickname correctly!

FRASIER

(1993–2004, NBC) A show so proud of its Seattle setting that the Space Needle is featured in its title logo, *Frasier* is the celebrated *Cheers* spin-off wherein a fussy divorced psychiatrist returns to his hometown to host a call-in radio show and reconnect with his family. Kelsey Grammer won four Emmys for his title role, David Hyde Pierce won four Emmys as Frasier's competitively fussy brother, and John Mahoney won zero Emmys playing the ex-cop dad (but was nominated twice). Over the course of *Frasier*'s eleven-season run, only one episode—"The 1000th Show"—was actually filmed in Seattle, with the vast majority of the show shot on perma-sets at Paramount Studios. Still, nearly every episode featured the eternally commented-upon apartment terrace view of the Space Needle—a view that exists from no actual building or apartment in Seattle but was constructed by the Hollywood dream factory to make *Frasier* (and Seattle) look glamorous. Despite the lack of boots on the ground, *Frasier* successfully captures something of the spirit of Seattle, a place of fine-art-loving germaphobes fluent in mental-health lingo, all hanging out at Café Nervosa.

BRAND UPON THE BRAIN!

(2006, DIR. GUY MADDIN)

Directed and co-written by renowned Canadian experimental filmmaker Guy Maddin, *Brand Upon the Brain!* is a silent film shot in and around Seattle with local actors and presented around the world with live narration, music, and Foley artists. Subtitled "A Remembrance in 12 Chapters," the film follows "Guy Maddin" (played by two actors) as he returns to the deserted island where he was raised and where his parents ran an orphanage. Things get strange with organ harvesting and oppressive memories, all presented like a lost silent film in black and white with big stagey acting, supertitles, and a poetically choppy editing. Crucial setting: the Point Wilson Lighthouse in Port Townsend, Washington. Available as part of the Criterion Collection.

BUSTIN' LOOSE

(1981, DIR. OZ SCOTT)

Capturing iconic comic Richard Pryor near the peak of his mainstream fame with the ever estimable Cicely Tyson as co-star, *Bustin' Loose* is a star packed garbage picture in which ex-con Pryor must assuage his parole officer by driving a bus full of special-needs orphans from Philadelphia to Washington State. Among the orphans are a preteen patricidal pyromaniac and a sexaholic Vietnamese tween who can't stop propositioning Pryor. En route, Pryor and orphan-wrangler Tyson fall in love, everyone has a hilarious time at a slapsticky Klan rally, and eventually this bus of misfits reaches their rural Washington destination, with scenes filmed in Carnation, Ellensburg, Snohomish, Redmond, and Seattle.

CAPTAIN FANTASTIC

(2016, DIR. MATT ROSS)

In the Washington wilderness, a father and his six children have been living off the grid for years in a plumbing-free utopia where the forest-schooled kids do book reports on *Guns, Germs, and Steel* and the family celebrates Noam Chomsky's birthday instead of Christmas. When family drama calls the tribe out of the woods and into structured society, things get dramatically complicated. Starring an Oscar-nominated Viggo Mortensen as the damaged-lefty dad, *Captain Fantastic* (not his real name) was made entirely in the Pacific Northwest, primarily in Western Washington: the Noam Chomsky Christmas goes down on a Snohomish riverbank, the emergency room scenes are at Kirkland's EvergreenHealth Medical Center, and the fiery finale was staged at Deception Pass State Park. Captured on film for all time: the legendary but shit-brained Uncle Sam billboard on I-5 North outside Chehalis, Washington.

THE CHANGELING

(1980, DIR. PETER MEDAK)

In this haunted-house classic, a recently widowed George C. Scott moves into a spooky-ass Seattle mansion, only to find mysterious running water, self-smashing mirrors, and a secret-packed house intent on avenging itself. Starring Seattle's Stimson-Green Mansion as the house that "doesn't want people," the film was primarily shot in British Columbia but features a ton of iconic Seattle establishing shots, including SeaTac Airport, University of Washington's Red Square, the Space Needle, the Rainier Tower, and the Lacey V. Murrow Memorial Bridge. Bonus: *The Changeling* features the film debut of Kyle MacLachlan, at the time a UW student who was paid $10 as an extra.

CINDERELLA LIBERTY

(1973, DIR. MARK RYDELL)

A gritty Seattle romance set almost entirely in downtown and Belltown, *Cinderella Liberty* stars a post-*Godfather* James Caan as a sailor on shore leave and an Oscar-nominated Marsha Mason as the streetwalking single mom who sparks his devotion. Set to an inventive jazz-funk score by John Williams (who worked as a jazz pianist before becoming a film composer), the film captures a Seattle that's all pawn shops, dive bars, and waterfront, where the perpetually outcast characters love, fuck, help, and disappoint one another. Key locales: Post Alley, Gas Works Park, and Pier 52's Colman Dock.

COME SEE THE PARADISE

(1990, DIR. ALAN PARKER)

Set before and during World War II, this lush period piece concerns an Irish American man (Dennis Quaid) who falls in love with a Japanese American woman (Tamlyn Tomita). Forbidden to wed in her native California, the young lovers flee to Seattle where interracial marriage is legal, and they start building a life together—until the bombing of Pearl Harbor, when this American bride is sent with her family to a series of internment facilities, ending up in a prison camp outside Manzanar, California. One of just a handful of films dealing with the internment of Japanese Americans during WWII, *Come See the Paradise* wraps its brutal facts in a romantic "Remember when?" framing device that makes the movie less a portrait of the brutal racism that flares up during times of fear and more a heartwarming tale of family survival. It's also packed with PNW locales. The old Portland Meadows racetrack was used as one of the "assembly centers," and the Portland railway station is the site of a mega-scene with five hundred period-dressed extras. Astoria stood in for California's Terminal Island, and the cannery scenes were filmed in the town of Cathlamet on the Washington coast.

PNW XXX

You might think that Pacific Northwesterners, with their sun-deprived hides, woolen socks, and seasonal affective disorder, might not be so game to fuck on film. You'd be wrong.

HUMP! FILM FESTIVAL

Hosted by syndicated sex-advice columnist and Seattleite Dan Savage, HUMP! is the annual amateur porn festival that "allows consenting adults to be porn stars for a weekend, not a lifetime." (Cell phones are forbidden at screenings and showcased videos are destroyed before the audience's eyes after the last show.) The result is a cornucopia of cinematic sex with something to enflame, shock, delight, and beguile everyone, performed by your fellow citizens. (As a HUMP! attendee, I once saw a movie where my former intern blew a guy in a Superman suit!)

THE LAST BATH

(1975, DIR. CHARLES STRAUMER) Directed by Seattle filmmaker Karl Krogstad under his one-off nom de porn Charles Straumer, *The Last Bath* is the Seattle-based hardcore film wherein a well-endowed man with photogenic junk and a houseboat wanders around in an acid-rock haze while encountering women who cannot stop performing fellatio on him. It's a freaky hippie fantasia with psychedelic film effects blending with horny goblin noises as our hero climaxes in slow motion. Like all good pornography, *The Last Bath* confronts suicide via a would-be jumper on the Aurora Bridge, briefly noted by our man on his way to an assignation. Then it's back to slurping.

SEATTLE BAREBACK BOYZ

In this gay porn series produced by GAE Boy Video, young, hairless, and markedly thin guys have sex without condoms in and around Seattle, from hotel rooms to woodsy outdoor areas. Shot amateur style with no framing narrative beyond "let's fuck without condoms," *Seattle Bareback Boyz* is a lean affair, but what it lacks in character development it makes up  in graphic action. Fun fact: a *Seattle Bareback Boyz* DVD was found in a suspect's car on one of Chris Hansen's predator-hunting TV shows, requiring Hansen to narrate the line, "in the car they found a DVD entitled *Seattle Bareback Boyz*."

CTHULHU

(2007, DIR. DANIEL GILDARK)

In this indie thriller, H. P. Lovecraft's fictional cosmic force Cthulhu is repurposed to power a tale of a bisexual man confronting the apocalypse on the Oregon coast. Crucial background info: the film's director and writer were filmmaking novices, the cast's big name was Tori Spelling (who showed up in a supporting role), and the result was a legendary mess that employed a slew of Seattle film artists, screened at the Seattle International Film Festival, then slunk off to die in the shadows. But out of such dung do flowers grow, and *Cthulhu* got a new lease on life with a 2009 DVD release featuring the still-not-good movie and an instantly legendary commentary track, on which director Gildark and screenwriter Grant Cogswell explain to the best of their abilities what made their attempt at filmmaking so not-good. Cogswell, in particular, goes after all the dumb ideas and failures of execution, describing the script as "a train wreck," mocking himself for trying to stage the apocalypse on an indie budget, and concluding that "there's about forty minutes in the middle that work as a movie." It's an invaluable behind-the-scenes exposé, created with the explicit aim of helping future low-budget filmmakers avoid similar pitfalls.

VANCOUVER SWITCHEROO

Looking for a famous Seattle-based film and not finding it in this book? You're likely a victim of the Vancouver Switcheroo, wherein a Seattle-set film is actually shot in nearby Vancouver, British Columbia, where the weather, light, and basic cityscape are similar, but film-production tax credits are far more substantial. Among the many Vancouver-for-Seattle switch-outs: the terrific Joseph Gordon-Levitt/Seth Rogen cancer comedy *50/50*, the terrible Al Pacino thriller *88 Minutes*, and the rain-drenched AMC series *The Killing*.

DAREDREAMER
(1989, DIR. BARRY CAILLIER)

Starring and featuring songs written and performed by Seattle children's entertainer Tim Noah, this aggressively kooky independent musical concerns Winston, a thirty-something high school student who can't complete a task without losing himself in a big musical fantasia. This happens over and over, with the staging of musical numbers spilling out of the school (portrayed by Shorecrest High) and into such Seattle venues as the Georgetown Steam Plant and the Seattle Underground tunnels, where teams of dancers (choreographed by Seattle's Wade Madsen) exert themselves in service of the goofiest story imaginable. It's a total stoner gawkfest, available in full (for now) on the internet.

Queer Cinema

Seattle is one of America's great gay cities—an early adopter of marriage equality, home to numerous LGBT notables (Sue Bird, Dan Savage, Brandi Carlile), and producer and supporter of an array of queer film.

CROCODILE TEARS (1997, DIR. TED SOD) In writer/director Ted Sod's black comedy, a man makes a deal with the devil to rid himself of HIV, unleashing a world of chaos. Featuring a bevy of Seattle queers (including Dan Savage, who co-stars and also juggles), the film situates crucial scenes at Capitol Hill's Bonney Watson funeral home and the Comedy Underground in Pioneer Square.

INLAWS & OUTLAWS (2005, DIR. DREW EMERY) Drew Emery's documentary is an oral history of love, as told by real-life lovers both gay and straight, with the intermingled orientations illuminating the cruelty of laws restricting marriage to heterosexuals. A crucial conversation starter en route to Washington State's passage of marriage equality in 2012.

TORREY PINES (2016, DIR. CLYDE PETERSEN) Based on a true story, this stop-motion animated feature follows a queer–punk kid growing up in the chaotic wake of a schizophrenic mother. Told with bold style, gorgeous DIY animation, and music by Kimya Dawson and filmmaker Petersen's band Your Heart Breaks.

THE JINKX & DELA HOLIDAY SPECIAL (2020, DIR. BENDELACREME) Filmed on a Seattle soundstage and then beamed around the globe via Hulu, this rollicking holiday special finds international drag stars (with Seattle roots) Jinkx Monsoon and BenDeLaCreme torching tradition, smoking out the Savior, and committing to ridiculous musical numbers to create a new holiday classic—one that receives seasonal big-screen showings across the country.

POTATO DREAMS OF AMERICA (2021, DIR. WES HURLEY) In this autobiographical fantasia, filmmaker Wes Hurley tells the story of his mother's journey (with young gay Wes in tow) from the Soviet Union to an arranged marriage in the United States. Featuring an award-winning performance by Lea DeLaria, this Russian/American dramedy was shot in and around Seattle, with the American scenes filmed at existing locations around the city and the Russian scenes shot on a soundstage housed in a former Staples.

DEAR LEMON LIMA

(2009, DIR. SUZI YOONESSI)

This charming indie film follows a thirteen-year-old half-Yup'ik girl navigating teenage life and love and oppressive tradition in Fairbanks, Alaska. In an unusual twist, Fairbanks is portrayed almost entirely by locations in western and central Washington, including Seattle and the city of Cashmere.

THE DETAILS

(2011, DIR. JACOB ESTES)

In this star-packed black comedy that nobody saw, Tobey Maguire is a Seattle ob-gyn who's married to Elizabeth Banks, boning Kerry Washington, and refuting the horny advances of Laura Linney— all while battling a raccoon infestation *and* exacting murderous revenge on his enemies! The performances are big and iffy, the plot is bonkers, and the Seattle-and-environs setting includes the Skagit River, Lake Union, and Queen Anne's Kerry Park.

DISCLOSURE

(1994, DIR. BARRY LEVINSON)

A sexual harassment thriller with an Ennio Morricone score, *Disclosure* pits Michael Douglas against Demi Moore in a battle for the truth of an inter-office sexual assault accusation. With Moore's character basically a praying mantis in a business suit, the film (based on Michael Crichton's novel) is something of a corporate *Fatal Attraction* with less murder and more surprisingly graphic oral sex between its movie-star leads. Set in Seattle in a perfectly Pioneer Square-y office building of metal, wood, and glass (the

KARL KROGSTAD

Media prankster, cinema provocateur, and a real-life character bigger than any in his movies, Seattle artist Karl Krogstad made over sixty films—long documentaries, short features, experimental music videos, found-footage fantasias, grotesque dreamscape narratives. These works screened at Northwest Film Forum, Portland Art Museum, and Seattle Art Museum, where he wasn't above yelling at his interlocutors during audience Q&As (see *The Autobiography of Karl Krogstad*, 2014). He was almost as well-known for his self-promotion, wheat-pasting "Karl Krogstad Makes Movies" posters all over town. (At one point, he even faced up to eleven years in jail for defacing street poles, bridges, and concrete monorail pillars. The case was eventually dismissed.) Throughout his career, Krogstad's films primarily employed volunteers, for whom his film sets were de facto film schools, with Krogstad grads eventually landing work on NW television projects like *Twin Peaks* and *Northern Exposure*. As for the films, they're all over the map, and can be found at Scarecrow Video.

set of which was constructed in the real Pioneer Square), the movie stumbles around in a men's-rights miasma while showcasing a number of prime local settings, including Volunteer Park, the Arboretum, Pike Place Market, Smith Tower, and the Bainbridge Island ferry.

DOGFIGHT

(1991, DIR. NANCY SAVOCA)

One of three, count 'em three, PNW films that River Phoenix
made in his abbreviated life, *Dogfight* is a 1960s period piece
tracking the romance between an eighteen-year-old Marine on
his way to Vietnam and a young woman (beautifully played by
Lili Taylor) who challenges him with her empathy, idealism, and
toughness. The film's first segment exploits a cruel framing device
(a "dogfight" is a party where Marines compete to bring the ugliest
date) before transitioning into a charming character study, as our
young couple runs around making the most of Phoenix's final night
before deployment. In a kicky twist, Seattle is cast as San Francisco,
with numerous Seattle locales (the Paramount Theatre, the Nitelite
Lounge, the Hotel Sorrento) popping up in *Dogfight*'s vision of
San Francisco. Bonuses: one of cinema's great listening-to-a-song
scenes (set to Dylan's "Don't Think Twice, It's Alright"), plus a baby
Brendan Fraser (at the time a student at Seattle's Cornish College
of the Arts) as Sailor #1 in the bar-fight scene.

DOUBLE JEOPARDY

(1999, DIR. BRUCE BERESFORD)

According to the "double jeopardy" clause in the US Constitution,
a person cannot be prosecuted twice for substantially the same
crime. According to Ashley Judd's character in *Double Jeopardy*,
this means she can legally kill the husband whom she was
convicted of killing but who faked his own death! Tommy Lee
Jones co-stars as the parole officer who actually understands the
law and would like to help. Shot primarily in British Columbia, with
a crucial opening segment shot on Washington's Whidbey Island.

EAST OF THE MOUNTAINS

(2021, DIR. S. J. CHIRO)

Seattle-based film actor Tom Skerritt has made a career of acing singular supporting roles in indelible films, from Robert Altman's *MASH* and Ridley Scott's *Alien* to *Top Gun* and *Steel Magnolias*. (Your author's favorite: 1977's *The Turning Point*.) He's also Seattle's most beloved hometown celebrity (non-sports division); a friendly, generous presence in Seattle's literary, film, and theater scenes; and a smiley gentleman out-and-about town. In Seattle-based filmmaker S. J. Chiro's *East of the Mountains*, Skerritt gets something that's previously eluded him: a big fat leading role of the present-in-virtually-every-scene variety. Based on the novel by PNW writer David Guterson and co-starring Oscar-winner Mira Sorvino, *East of the Mountains* casts Skerritt as a retired surgeon confronting his mortality on a road trip back to his childhood home east of the Cascades in Washington State. It's a beautiful, quiet, but very alive film, most of which was shot in Eastern Washington (including parts of the Columbia Plateau), with additional filming in Seattle's Ballard and Wallingford neighborhoods.

ENOUGH

(2002, DIR. MICHAEL APTED)

Jennifer Lopez stars as a wife and mother who flees her abusive husband to hide in the Pacific Northwest, where she cuts her hair, learns Krav Maga, and turns her body into a weapon for daughter-protection and revenge. The plot-and-star combo seems like a slam dunk, but thanks to its overwhelming crassness and parade of laughable plot points, *Enough* wound up inspiring brutal mockery. "It's a loathsome movie, it really is and it makes absolutely no sense," said Richard Roeper on *At the Movies*. "All this to protect a helium-voiced little girl with whom Lopez has so little chemistry, it's as if she's handling garbage rather than a small child," wrote Alice King in *Entertainment Weekly*. Still, the movie captures some ace PNW locales, including a glistening, sun-drenched Puget Sound, Gig Harbor's old-timey gas station Rosedale Market, and Orcas Island's West Sound, presented as the fictional seaport where Lopez finds refuge and the fire within.

THE FABULOUS BAKER BOYS
(1989, DIR. STEVE KLOVES)

In rain-soaked, late-eighties Seattle, a lounge act composed of piano-playing brothers joins forces with an up-and-coming singer in hopes of paying their bills and achieving their career dreams, and then . . . life unfolds. There's lots of music, but the movie's not a musical. There are romantic sparks, but it's not a love story. Instead, it's a story about relationships—*working* relationships, focusing on shared labor, even when dealing with brothers and their potential love interests, and it's all strikingly, affectingly life-sized. Jeff Bridges and Beau Bridges star as the brothers surfing a shared lifetime of resentment, competition, and artistic entwinement, and Michelle Pfeiffer gives an awards-magnet of a performance as an achingly ambitious, respectably talented vocal performer who spends a few seasons in the Baker brothers' orbit.

Filmed primarily in Los Angeles (?!), the movie still feels spiritually true to Seattle, which is rendered, as *Slant Magazine*'s Chuck Bowen wrote, "as a surreal realm that appears to have been ported in nearly unchanged from the backlots of the thrillers and studio musicals of the 1930s and 1940s." Among the actual Seattle settings: Ivar's Acres of Clams, the Fairmont Olympic Hotel's Starlite Lounge, and Pioneer Square. (Fair warning/total bummer: in the first minutes, a character makes a shocking racist proclamation about Seattle's jazz scene and is allowed to just walk away, instead of being tarred and feathered before our eyes.)

NORTHERN EXPOSURE

(1990-1995, CBS) This acclaimed dramedy series tracks the kooky residents—fish-out-of-water doctor! philosophical radio DJ! sexy bush pilot!—of the fictional town of Cicely, Alaska. But the whole damn thing was shot in Roslyn, Washington, eighty-three miles southeast of Seattle, where familiar *Northern Exposure* sights abound on the town's main drag, from Central Sundries (the store owned by town elder Ruth-Anne) and the Brick tavern to the camel painting adorning the outside wall of the Roslyn Cafe.

FEAR

(1996, DIR. JAMES FOLEY)

Described by producer Brian Grazer as *"Fatal Attraction* for teens," *Fear* stars Reese Witherspoon as a Seattle high schooler who falls in love with an edgy, mysterious new student (Mark Wahlberg), only to have him wreck her life out of jealousy and whatever mental illness gives you superhuman revenge capabilities and a weird Boston accent. There's some creepy "The Girl Is Mine" competition between Marky Mark and Daddy Dad (William Petersen), and the threat of Witherspoon's blooming sexuality eventually endangers her whole family, requiring mom Amy Brenneman to defend her brood with a power drill. Despite being largely shot in Vancouver, *Fear* gets the feel of Seattle right, from the opening-credits shot of the Kingdome to the rich, fit dad excited for the James Taylor show at the Pier. In the movie's best scene, Witherspoon is fingered on a roller coaster, climaxing just in time for the big drop. Every Seattleite sincerely wants this scene to have been shot at Seattle Center's legendary Fun Forest, but alas, it's Vancouver's Playland amusement park.

FRANCES

(1982, DIR. GRAEME CLIFFORD)

Born in Seattle in 1913, the actress Frances Farmer earned a seemingly permanent place in America's imagination after a thoroughly Northwest early life: After graduating from West Seattle High School, she paid her way through the University of Washington working as a singing waitress at Mount Rainier National Park. Then came New York, Broadway, Hollywood, stardom, infamy, and an aggressive mental illness that would see her institutionalized at Western State Hospital in Steilacoom, Washington.

continued...

KURT COBAIN

Nothing retroactively suffuses a life with meaning like suicide, and thanks to his beauty, artistic brilliance, famous wife, and premature end, Kurt Cobain has provided regular inspiration for filmmakers. Here's the good, bad, and ugly of Cobain cinema.

KURT & COURTNEY (1998, DIR. NICK BROOMFIELD) A tabloid-level documentary that strains to float the notion that Courtney Love may have had a hand in the death of Kurt Cobain, *Kurt & Courtney* is a garbage parade, full of the flimsiest what-ifs and if-you-say-so mysteries. Still, it looks like a masterwork next to *Soaked in Bleach* (2015, dir. Benjamin Statler), another "Was Kurt killed?" rumor puzzle, with *Unsolved Mysteries*–quality reenactments and edits so manipulative the film was denounced by its interview subjects. Comedy gold!

LAST DAYS (2005, DIR. GUS VAN SANT) Gus Van Sant's slow, spare feature tracks the decline of a junkie musician whose sock-monkey puppets and soggy blonde locks peg him as Cobain. (Actor Michael Pitt bears a spooky likeness.) Shot in New York's Hudson Valley with film stock treated to suggest the misty PNW, the film wanders to its subject's inevitable but unseen end, spending time on the minutia—Mormons at the door, a phone always ringing somewhere—that fills the days of a guy on his way out.

KURT COBAIN: ABOUT A SON (2006, DIR. A. J. SCHNACK) Cobain is presented via audio from his interviews with Michael Azerrad, author of the Nirvana bio *Come as You Are*. Bracing in edited text, here Cobain's unedited insights come wrapped in his rambling junkie whine, which plays over "corresponding" images of a disorienting randomness. For fetishists only.

COBAIN: MONTAGE OF HECK (2015, DIR. BRETT MORGEN) The only Cobain documentary produced with his family's okay, *Montage* makes powerful use of its subject's art, with Kurt's ballpoint sketches brought to animated life over alternate takes of his songs. The first half cements the legend of childhood trauma and artistic aspiration, while the second introduces the genius junkie and shitty dad. "The second half, we all ended up hating Kurt," said Frances Bean Cobain, Kurt's daughter and executive producer of the doc, to the *Independent*. "We were all like, 'You whiny little bitch.'" (For those craving a film experience that captures a Cobain worthy of admiration forever, watch Nirvana's set on *MTV Unplugged*.)

This 1982 biopic stars Jessica Lange as the brilliant but doomed Farmer, and draws upon the contested biography *Shadowland*, which fictionalizes history in depicting Farmer as having undergone a partial lobotomy in the 1950s. (It's not factual, but Lange's portrayal of Farmer's ghost-brained chilliness after this non-existent lobotomy certainly helped earn her the Oscar for Best Actress.) The film is a bit of a slog, feeling at times as if we're walking through her life in real time, but the slow pace makes the freak-out surprises really pop. Among the caught-on-film Seattle hallmarks: the Paramount Theatre (which hosted a big Frances Farmer film premiere in both real life and on film) and a normal amount of drizzly Seattle rain (the kind you keep away with a light jacket and beret).

GEORGIA
(1995, DIR. ULU GROSBARD)

Built around a fearless performance by Jennifer Jason Leigh, the Seattle-based drama *Georgia* charts the twisty relationship between Leigh's punky, drug-addicted barroom singer Sadie and her successful folk-singer sister Georgia (Mare Winningham, in an Oscar-nominated performance). It's a day-by-day character study exploring talent, luck, and family, kept rolling with a powerful supporting cast. Ted Levine (aka *Silence of the Lamb*'s Buffalo Bill) is Georgia's sweet husband/Sadie's perpetually supportive brother-in-law, X's John Doe fronts the bar band that takes Sadie as its singer, and John C. Reilly stumbles around as a junkie drummer. (The movie takes pains to show exactly how boring junkiedom is.) Featuring musical performances in a number of Seattle bars, the movie climaxes with a show at the Seattle Opera house, where the beloved and professional Georgia invites scrappy Sadie to perform a song with her band—inspiring Jennifer Jason Leigh to deliver a grueling, groveling performance of Van Morrison's "Take Me Back" that goes on forever, at the end of which she is thoroughly debased. Some find the performance brilliant, others think it ventures into Joker territory, but it's definitely something to see once.

Megan Griffiths

From artsy mood pieces to rollicking rom-coms, the work of Seattle filmmaker Megan Griffiths has confirmed her stature as one of PNW cinema's most diverse talents.

THE OFF HOURS (2011) One of your author's very favorite PNW movies, *The Off Hours* is writer/director Griffiths lackadaisical exploration of the small community gathered around a western Washington truck stop. More than anything, it's an exploration of a state of being—a passive state of being, when you take your feet off the pedals of your life and just coast. Griffiths turns this state of being into a physical place, creating a world that flirts with dreamscape-iness but is rooted in hard real life thanks to an instantly grounding lead performance by Amy Seimetz.

LUCKY THEM (2013) Leaving lyrically static dreamscapes behind, Griffiths applies herself to a script by Huck Botko and Emily Wachtel. *Lucky Them* follows a forty-something music journalist tasked with hunting down a rock star who killed himself, but maybe didn't, and is also her ex. Toni Collette gives a cumulatively astonishing performance in the lead, Thomas Haden Church co-stars as a rich jackass who joins her on her journey, and things climax with the surprise appearance of a humungo-star (whose name might rhyme with Bonnie Blep). Among the featured Seattle locales: the Belltown bar Rob Roy, the Capitol Hill pizzeria Big Mario's, and the cleanest Pioneer Square you'll ever see.

SADIE (2018) Leaving poppy dramedy behind, Griffiths wrote and directed this quiet character study set in an Everett trailer park where thirteen-year-old Sadie (Sophia Mitri Schloss) yearns for her deployed father while waging cold war against her too-present mother (Melanie Lynskey, terrific as ever). It's a beautiful exploration of the stories the powerless tell about the powerful to make sense of the world, and how the powerful have no clue what havoc they leave in their wake.

GRASSROOTS

(2003, DIR. STEPHEN GYLLENHAAL)

If you are reading this book in order, you'll have already seen the name Grant Cogswell, the novice screenwriter behind the flop NW thriller *Cthulhu* and the star of the instructively self-lacerating filmmaker commentary on the *Cthulhu* DVD. A few years before diving into a low-budget Lovecraft adaptation, Cogswell undertook another hugely ambitious endeavor—running for Seattle City Council on a platform that aimed to solve Seattle's transit problems by expanding the city's Monorail. Running Cogswell's campaign was Phil Campbell, a journalist who afterwards wrote a book about the experience, and this film is the cinematic adaptation of Campbell's account of working to get a true political outsider—a tireless ranter with big emotions, no less—elected in a city that just might be unconventional enough to go for it.

Shot all over Seattle (including a scene featuring the desk of yours truly at the newsweekly the *Stranger*), *Grassroots* is a road-to-the-election dramedy starring Jason Biggs, Joel David Moore, and Cedric the Entertainer, plus a ton of Seattle landmarks, including Re-bar (home of both the actual and fictional election-night watch party), Broadway Performance Hall, Phinney Ridge Neighborhood Association, and KOMO 4 news reporter Connie Thompson. Fun historical fact: while Cogswell lost his bid for City Council, his dream of an expanded urban railway was realized five years later with Sound Transit's Link Light Rail.

THE HAND THAT ROCKS THE CRADLE

(1992, DIR. CURTIS HANSON)

In this suburban psychological thriller, a Seattle family's perfect life is upended by a nanny harboring a secret and a heart full of vengeance. Rebecca De Mornay stars as the whack nanny who icily exploits her host family's vulnerabilities (asthma, infants, sexy exes) in an attempt to wreck everything they love. Annabella Sciorra co-stars as the family's besieged mother, Julianne Moore provides crucial support as the husband's sexy ex, and it's all awash in recognizable Seattle stuff, from the Volunteer Park Conservatory to old-school Metro busses and Windermere Real Estate signs. (In addition to Seattle, filming took place in Issaquah and Tacoma, the latter being the site of the troubled family's residence.) More than any other film I watched for this book, this one best captures Seattle's particular grayness, with the low skies and vast clouds creating the type of interior dimness that requires lamps in the middle of the day. The movie's also awash in weirdly gendered suffering, with female characters withstanding obstetrical gropings, punitive miscarriages, and vengeful breastfeedings. In the end, things are resolved, as they often are in suburbia, by a well-placed white picket fence.

HARRY AND THE HENDERSONS

(1987, DIR. WILLIAM DEAR)

What if E.T. and Chewbacca had a giant hairy baby that moved in with a Seattle family and taught them to love and cherish nature? This is the question behind *Harry and the Hendersons*, in which a Bigfoot/Sasquatch character is adopted by John Lithgow's family, with comedically chaotic results. While the humans fuss over keeping their new houseguest a secret, Harry rocks out in the Henderson home—channel-surfing in the La-Z-Boy, and

continued ...

Harry and the
Hendersons

smuggling fur coats and meat products out of the house for burial in the backyard. (The movie's a bit of a vegetarian screed, a meat-free *Mac and Me*.) When a confused Harry flees the Henderson home, a good old-fashioned hunt for Bigfoot commences, with the Hendersons' quest to save their cherished friend competing with local hunters' quests to blast Sasquatch. Winner of the Oscar for Best Makeup, the movie was shot almost entirely in the Puget Sound region, including North Cascades National Park, I-90 near the town of Index, Kachess Lake, North Bend, and Okanogan-Wenatchee National Forest, as well as Seattle's Wallingford, Ballard, and Beacon Hill neighborhoods.

HARRY IN YOUR POCKET

(1973, DIR. BRUCE GELLER)

In this grimy crime thriller, a team of professional pickpockets live and love and seize pocket contents in early-seventies Seattle. James Coburn operates a de facto pickpocket school on the downtown streets, training a team of newbies in parks and on sidewalks around Seattle, then celebrating in their swanky waterfront hotel. (For Harry's crew, everything is first class, with fine living the first line of defense against suspicion.) The pickpockets flirt by pickpocketing each other, the crew leaves Seattle behind for Salt Lake City, and eventually mistakes are made that bring it all crashing down. Featuring a cameo by then-mayor of Seattle Wes Uhlman!

HIGHWAY

(2002, DIR. JAMES COX)

Originally titled *A Leonard Cohen Afterworld* after a line in Nirvana's "Pennyroyal Tea," this in-your-face, straight-to-DVD road trip fantasia stars Jared Leto, Jake Gyllenhaal, and Selma Blair as misfits who flee their troubled Vegas lives and wind up on a cross-country road trip. The trip climaxes in Seattle at the

continued...

Lynn Shelton

At age 37, Lynn Shelton was editing other people's films and dreaming of making her own but worried she'd aged past the starting date for new directors. Then Shelton saw Claire Denis speak at Northwest Film Forum, where the revered French director mentioned she'd made her first film at forty—and Shelton got to work. Honing a specific method of cinematic storytelling built upon improvised dialogue, idiosyncratic performances, and seemingly stumbled-upon moments of rich, hilarious humanity, Shelton distinguished herself with a run of movies set and shot in the Pacific Northwest.

WE GO WAY BACK (2006) In Shelton's debut, a young woman adrift in adulthood is called to shake up her static life by her thirteen-year-old self, who appears via letters and, through some sort of mumblecore magical realism, in person. It's fucking audacious, and Shelton and her cast make it work with the uncannily lived-in, life-sized feel that was part of her cinematic world from the start. Winner of the Grand Jury Prize at Slamdance 2006, as well as the Vision Award for Cinematography bestowed upon Shelton's crucial DP Benjamin Kasulke.

MY EFFORTLESS BRILLIANCE (2008) Two guys—one artsy, one woodsy—process a rupture in their friendship, commencing a foot-in-mouth parade that feels repetitive and basic after the complex twists of her debut. Still, it was a crucial step en route to . . .

HUMPDAY (2009) Made for less than $20,000 over ten days in Seattle and landing before dazzled audiences at Sundance and Cannes, Shelton's breakthrough is a face-clutchingly funny film about a man torn between his sane and loving wife and his dumb bohemian friend, with whom he has agreed to make a pornographic film. Shelton's aim for revelatory moments has sharpened, her dialogue-improvising cast—led by Mark Duplass, Joshua Leonard, and Alycia Delmore—keeps things fresh and shocking, and the low-key thrilling result won the Special Jury Prize at the 2009 Sundance Film Festival.

YOUR SISTER'S SISTER (2011) Another drifty, revelatory mingling of humans, in which Emily Blunt and Rosemarie DeWitt tussle with Mark Duplass over love and parenthood in the San Juan Islands. The script is another improvised-dialogue gem, Shelton and Kasulke continue to make the most of the region's impertinent dampness and low gray skies.

TOUCHY FEELY (2013) Starring Rosemarie DeWitt as a massage therapist with a sudden aversion to bodily contact, *Touchy Feely* is a little film that takes big risks with a near-ambient plot that attempts to draw drama from internal processes. The cast of seasoned stars—Elliot Page, Allison Janney, Ron Livingston—commits to their weird little corner of this world, as does the relative newbie Tomo Nakayama, a beloved PNW singer/songwriter who makes his film debut as Elliot Page's angel-voiced love interest.

LAGGIES (2014) In Shelton's first film with a script by someone else (Andrea Seigel), Keira Knightley stars as a woman whose existential crisis drives her to befriend and eventually move in with a high-school girl (Chloe Grace Moretz) and her sad single dad (Sam Rockwell). Knightley gives a good, raw performance, but too many plot points are ludicrous.

OUTSIDE IN (2017) Shelton's first full-on drama stars Jay Duplass as an ex-con transitioning back to life in rural western Washington and Edie Falco as his key post-prison supporter. Under misty green-gray skies, our hero shuffles through his days—learning computer stuff, looking for work, seeing his parole officer—until new romance and old grievances usher in the mumblecore fireworks. A seriously lovely film, it was shot all around Snohomish and Granite Falls.

memorial for the recently departed Kurt Cobain, where a sea of sad, beflanneled kids with paper-cup candles mill about Seattle Center's International Fountain. But prior to the film's final eighteen minutes, *Highway* is a grating parade of kooky scenes and Olympic-level overacting. (See: *Scrubs*'s John C. McGinley, who yells from under dreadlocks.)

HIT!
(1973, DIR. SIDNEY J. FURIE)

In the opening segment of *Hit!*, a young woman in downtown Seattle follows a man into his car. The pimpish man puts a syringe into her arm, delivering a fatal overdose. We soon learn this young woman was the daughter of Federal Agent Nick Allen (played by Billy Dee Williams), who swears vengeance on not just the drug ring that killed his daughter but the whole drug cartel. To this end, he enlists a team of vengeance soldiers drawn from "normal life," each of whom bears a deep personal connection to the ravages of addiction and the drug trade and is mad enough to kill. It's a terrific conceit, allowing rich backstories—two of the drafted assassins are an old married couple still furious over their daughter's addiction and deadly overdose and still guilty over how they handled what they now see was an illness. (The movie has a sweet empathy-for-junkies moral.) As the web of assassination plots activates, the story moves beyond Seattle to points across the US. Along for the ride: Richard Pryor, who does great work as a sensitive widower roped into Williams's scheme. Besides Seattle, *Hit!* also features scenes shot in Gig Harbor and Port Hadlock, Washington.

HOUSE OF GAMES
(1987, DIR. DAVID MAMET)

One of the best-ever Seattle films, *House of Games* is writer/director David Mamet's con-game masterpiece starring Lindsay Crouse as a psychologist who invites herself into the shady world of professional con man Joe Mantegna, inspiring a head-spinning rush of set-ups, fake-outs, and betrayals. Set in a creepy nighttime Seattle centered around downtown and Belltown, where pool halls (the 211 Club!), bars (Charlie's Tavern) and hotels (Hotel Vintage) draw travelers and criminal dreamers, the movie glides along on its own subtle, life-sized magic until it all blows up in our faces. "I have seen so many films that were sleepwalking through the debris of old plots and second-hand ideas," wrote Roger Ebert in his four-star review. "This movie is awake." Along with tons of downtown locales, there's a crucial scene outside the art deco PacMed Building on Beacon Hill (later to become Amazon headquarters until 2010) and a serious showdown at Sea-Tac Airport.

THE IMMACULATE CONCEPTION OF LITTLE DIZZLE

(2009, DIR. DAVID RUSSO)

This one-of-a-kind movie from Seattle filmmaker David Russo concerns a young Seattle man who takes a job as a janitor for a mysterious cleaning company, instigating a slow-burn mystery involving pregnant men, evil corporate experiments, and "self-heating warm cookies that make [you] feel better." Russo has a storytelling style all his own, and a truly cinematic imagination. From plot-forwarding visuals and wittily compressed backstories to surprise bursts of animation, *Little Dizzle* never stops being inventive, almost exhaustively so, which somehow feels true to the overwhelming experience of our hero. Featuring a great supporting performance from Natasha Lyonne and a different view of the city than typically seen (rocky waterfront beaches, weird steep hills).

IT HAPPENED AT THE WORLD'S FAIR

(1963, DIR. NORMAN TAUROG)

Fresh out of the military and focusing on his film career, Elvis Presley made twenty-seven movies during the 1960s, nearly all of them corny musical comedies that critics hated and audiences ate up. *It Happened at the World's Fair* is no exception. Presley stars as a freelance crop duster who takes time out of his sexually-harassing-women-from-biplanes schedule to hitchhike to Seattle, where he assumes custody of a stranger's seven-year-old daughter for a day, and together they tour the Seattle World's Fair. Presley also sings ten whole damn songs and is perpetually macking on a parade of women who are all hairdos, breasts, and mincing steps. Still, the day at the fair is pretty thrilling, touring the famous Century 21 exhibit and featuring a reveal of the Space Needle so ravishing you will applaud from the comfort of your own home. Other local delights photographed all Hollywood-pretty: the Monorail, the Seattle Center fountain, and the blue-purple sky over the Sound at dusk.

KIMI

(2021, DIR. STEVEN SODERBERGH)

Made during the Great Covid Lockdown of 2020, Steven Soderbergh's physically restricted thriller concerns a work-from-home tech analyst who finds herself mired in a deadly conspiracy after unlocking the dirty secrets of an Alexa-like "electronic assistant." Something of a 21st-century spin on *Rear Window*, *KIMI* traps our voyeuristic heroine Zoe Kravitz at home not through a broken leg but acute agoraphobia, which she must conquer to battle the forces of evil. Set in a recognizable, appropriately grimy Pioneer Square, bustling with food trucks and office space and destination Thai restaurants, *KIMI* captures overcast Seattle perfectly, with key scenes filmed at Westlake Park (the protest over so-called "Homeless Safe Zones") and onboard a Sound Transit train. (The majority of interiors, however, are products of California soundstages.)

THE LAST MIMZY

(2007, DIR. ROBERT SHAYE)

In this family-friendly sci-fi adventure, a young brother and sister find a box of toys on the beach of Whidbey Island and all hell breaks loose. First, the kids develop supernatural powers and weird brain talents, which, when used, make all sorts of delightful inter-galaxy communication possible. However, such communications also trigger government sensors for potential nuclear terrorism?! Starring Timothy Hutton and Joely Richardson as the parents raising these trippy kids in a house in the Queen Anne neighborhood, the film shares some thematic elements with page 51's *Little Buddha* (the potential Tibetan destiny of Seattle kids) and features this bit of double-edged dialogue: "Why would terrorists attack Seattle?" "We got Boeing, Microsoft, the Music Experience . . ."

LATE AUTUMN

(2010, DIR. KIM TAE-YONG)

Co-produced by South Korea, China, and the US, *Late Autumn* is
a beguiling English-language drama detailing the transformative
Seattle adventure of an immigrant Chinese woman given a
seventy-two-hour parole from prison and the South Korean hustler
devoted to making her weekend of freedom mean something.
Tang Wei stars as Anna, incarcerated in Washington State for
the manslaughter of her abusive husband (John Woo, shown in
flashback) and given temporary leave to attend the Seattle funeral
of her mother. Hyun Bin co-stars as the hustler-on-the-run Hoon.
Together he and Anna embark on a situational romance with a hard
deadline à la Richard Linklater's *Before Sunrise*, but *Late Autumn*
has a dreaminess all its own. As our hard-luck pair wanders around
downtown Seattle—strolling through Pike Place Market, taking
the Market Ghost Tour, riding the damn Ducks—they get to know
the facts of one another. By the time they reach Seattle Center's
Fun Forest amusement park, things have grown dreamy, with the
partially dismantled amusement park providing the setting for a
surprise modern dance sequence between our two leads. The
movie's ultimate message gets yelled out by the Ride the Ducks
tour guide: "Enjoy the sun now, fog will come back!"

LIFE OR SOMETHING LIKE IT

(2002, DIR. STEPHEN HEREK)

Three years after her Oscar win for *Girl, Interrupted*, Angelina Jolie
threw all her movie-star power at this romantic dramedy in which a
Seattle television reporter's can-do career-gal life path is disrupted
by a seemingly random encounter with a would-be street prophet.
Jolie is our questioning reporter, Tony Shalhoub is the portentous
blurter, Edward Burns is Jolie's brown-haired love interest, and the

whole thing unfolds in a Seattle that any late-nineties/early-aughts city-dweller will recognize, from Elliott Bay Books and Safeco Field to "KQMO-TV," the news station played by Seattle's own KOMO-TV with a little added squiggle. (Among the KOMO-reporter cameos: Dan Lewis, Margo Myers, Steve Pool, and Theron Zahn.) In the movie's most memorable and embarrassing scene, Jolie's newscaster shows up drunk to report on the brewing showdown between Seattle police and striking transit workers—only to lead the strikers in an impromptu singalong of the Rolling Stones' "Satisfaction" and emerge a star! It's awful and should not be missed.

LITTLE BUDDHA
(1993, DIR. BERNARDO BERTOLUCCI)

The Italian director Bernardo Bertolucci conquered the world and the Oscars with his sprawling, meticulous *The Last Emperor* in 1987. Coming half a decade later, Bertolucci's *Little Buddha* is a more modest biopic affair with a plot split in two: In cold, gray Seattle, married couple Bridget Fonda and Chris Isaak are visited by Tibetan Buddhist monks who proclaim their young son to have a one-in-three chance of being a reincarnated Lama. As Fonda and her son investigate this prospect through a Tibetan Buddhist story book, the tales come to life in a ravishing Buddhist wonderland where a heavily made-up Keanu Reeves strikes Siddhartha poses, and the life story of the pre-Buddha is brought to stagey cinematic life. Visually it's striking, alternating between the insistent gray-green of Seattle and the lush orange explosion of the Siddhartha scenes, and Keanu Reeves's beauty and inherent woodenness find a happy home in the declamatory reenactments. As for Seattle angles: a couple of lovely scenes were filmed at Sakya Monastery in Seattle's Greenwood neighborhood, and the beautiful glassy house that architect Chris Isaak built for his family is on Queen

continued ...

Anne. (This is the second cinematic instance of a Seattle architect building his dream home; see also *Fear,* page 35.) Real-life fact: three years after *Little Buddha* hit cinemas, a Seattle four-year-old was actually chosen as the reincarnation of Lama Deschund Rinpoche and exported to Nepal for Lama training!

LOVE HAPPENS
(2009, DIR. BRANDON CAMP)

The title of this star-encrusted romantic dramedy appears to be a play on the phrase "Shit happens," only instead of shit, it's love, which makes it romantic. Aaron Eckhart stars as a widowed writer touring with his hit coping-with-loss book, and Jennifer Aniston co-stars as a quirky Seattle florist in a knit cap who reawakens his libido and heals his heart. As co-writer and Seattleite Mike Thompson told Mónica Guzmán at the *Seattle Post-Intelligencer*, the film strives to be a "valentine to Seattle," which is showcased through a parade of classic totems (Gum Wall, Fremont Troll, Elephant Car Wash, Bruce Lee's grave, rain) and one quirky date wherein Aniston commandeers a hydraulic repair bucket to hoist Eckhart into the air to peek in on a Rogue Wave show at Qwest Field. But there's no escaping the fact that Eckhart and Aniston are both bland with a capital *ZZZZZ*; there is no chemistry, only harmonious wardrobes.

MAD LOVE
(1995, DIR. ANTONIA BIRD)

High-drama mental illness is a recurring theme in PNW cinema, with characters ranging from official DSM-V poster children (Mary Stuart Masterson in *Benny & Joon*, Jessica Lange's *Frances*) to undiagnosed revenge monkeys (Rebecca De Mornay in *The Hand That Rocks the Cradle*, Marky Mark in *Fear*). In the romantic drama *Mad Love*, Drew Barrymore plays a high-school girl whose sparkly funness, fun sparkliness, and habit of setting off the school's fire alarm during the SATs paint her as bipolar. Chris O'Donnell co-stars as her love interest, and eventually, the impulsive young lovers steal a car and hit the road, where Barrymore unravels to the point that O'Donnell realizes that she is not crazy/sexy/cool but dangerously mentally ill. (There is a nerve-racking scene of covered-eyes highway driving that still makes my butthole clench.) Prior to the road trip, the movie is devoted to the PNW, with Nirvana's "Love Buzz" playing over the opening credits, many scenes at Sammamish High School, and, in a key courtship moment, O'Donnell presenting Barrymore with tickets to a 7 Year Bitch show. (However, the film fails the UW pronunciation test, going with the full "You Double-U.")

McQ
(1974, DIR. JOHN STURGES)

In this endlessly mockable conservative fantasia McQ, Seattle is a lawless hellpit where crime rules, cops are for target practice, and the only person who can fix this shit is sixty-seven-year-old John Wayne in a lime green Trans Am. When he's not stomping hippies or gunning down suspects, John Wayne's pre-corpse lives on a boat and says things like, "I'm up to my butt in gas!" Nevertheless, this celebration of police brutality and can-do senior living makes great use of Seattle, from the Dr. Jose P. Rizal Bridge and a Sonics game at Key Arena to the centerpiece car chase through the streets of downtown.

MY LAST YEAR WITH THE NUNS
(2014, DIR. BRET FETZER)

Based on the acclaimed stage show written and performed by Matt Smith, *My Last Year with the Nuns* recounts a rich, fraught stretch of Seattle history from the perspective of a 1960s teen attending St. Joseph School on north Capitol Hill. The film blends first-person storytelling and documentary to craft a high-school reminiscence that has something to say about childhood and

continued...

Seattle's seriously racist past. The team is loaded with local Seattle talent, from camera operator John Jeffcoat (director of the hit *Outsourced*) to cinematographer Benjamin Kasulke to animator Clyde Petersen.

AN OFFICER AND A GENTLEMAN
(1982, DIR. TAYLOR HACKFORD)

Lodged in the collective cinematic imagination for its swoony factory-floor finale set to a soaring "Up Where We Belong," this tough romantic drama stars Richard Gere as a sailor working his way through the Navy's Officer Candidate School, Debra Winger as the Puget Sound Deb who wins his heart, and Louis Gossett Jr. as the gunnery sergeant whose inspired yelling earned him an Oscar. It's all thoroughly Northwesty, with the bulk of filming occurring in Port Townsend on the Olympic Peninsula, from the training camp at Fort Worden (where the decompression chamber set remains in the building's basement) to the Tides Motel, where the "Officer and a Gentleman Suite" in which Gere and Winger go bang is available for rent.

OLD GOATS
(2011, DIR. TAYLOR GUTERSON)

Shot on Bainbridge Island on a $5,000 budget (!), this charming slice-of-life comedy stars three senior citizens playing lightly fictionalized versions of themselves, resulting in a near-documentary feel that adds up to something funny, perceptive, and one of a kind. A sort of time-reversed *Stand By Me* shot on a microbudget, *Old Goats* follows our senior-citizen friends as they navigate their post-retirement lives, from being thrown into close daily contact with longtime spouses to undertaking bucket list adventures to old-age dating. The largely non-professional actors

continued...

give good, sweet, knowing performances across the board, and the film captures something true and deep about lifelong friendships where elderly men turn into little boys in each other's presence. In a most happy-making development, this tiny movie found a big audience, making a splash at film festivals across the US and in Canada. Among the Bainbridge locales: Pegasus Coffee House, Island Fitness, and Eagle Harbor Book Co.

THE PAPER TIGERS

(2020, DIR. TRAN QUOC BAO)

What an effing delight! *The Paper Tigers* is the Seattle-shot and -set martial arts comedy in which a trio of former kung-fu prodigies reconnect in middle age to avenge the death of their childhood master. Built around big, plot-forwarding fight scenes—alongside segments of our dad-bod protagonists prepping for big, plot-forwarding fight scenes—*The Paper Tigers* is willing to send its movie camera flying through the air to keep you entertained. It also makes use of a whole bunch of Seattle's International District, with appearances by Hing Hay Park, Wing Luke Museum, Mak Fai Kung Fu Club, Nisei Veterans Committee Memorial Hall, and numerous beloved restaurants (Dynasty Room, Tai Tung, King's Barbecue House).

THE PARALLAX VIEW

(1974, DIR. ALAN J. PAKULA)

Lots of Seattle movies establish their locales with shots of the Space Needle, the observation tower built at Seattle Center for the 1962 World's Fair. *The Parallax View* one-ups everyone by setting a key early scene inside the Space Needle's glamorous observation-deck restaurant, where the political fundraiser that will inspire the rest of this twisty political thriller is going down. It is there where a pair of party guests—an assassin and his pursuer—

escape onto the goddamn TOP OF THE SPACE NEEDLE, punching it out six hundred feet in the air on the observation deck's sloped roof, until one of them AIEEEEEEEs and the film begins. Warren Beatty stars as the national reporter investigating the assassination who discovers an international web of corruption, and it's all very smart and thrilling with great noir-y dialogue and brilliant cinematography by DP Gordon Willis. But for our purposes, it's mostly about that killer opening scene. Bonus: shots of a Seattle parade featuring the Filipino Youth Activities dance team (the superstars of every Seattle parade ever), and a scene shot at the Gorge Dam on the Skagit River.

THE REAL WORLD:
SEATTLE

(1998, MTV) In MTV's pioneering smash, seven strangers share a house rigged with cameras and crewmembers to record their every move and edit it into something resembling a television program. In its seventh season, the show sent its strangers to Seattle, where they took up residence on Elliott Bay's Pier 70, worked as "modulators" at the radio station 107.7 The End, and flew to Nepal on REI's dime to wash elephants. They also weathered the disdain of Seattleites, many of whom considered the show a tacky, trend-jumping nuisance. ("Seattle says: The Real World sucks!" read a popular T-shirt.) But for *Real World* fans, the Seattle season is forever treasured for its avalanche of drama, including Irene's lyme disease, Stephen's "Am I gay?" fluctuations, and The Slap, the first time verbal provocations inspired real-world physical violence on the series.

TWIN PEAKS

Twin Peaks is the brain-twisting mystery series that brought cinema auteur David Lynch to primetime television, introduced America to the glory of Snoqualmie Falls and accessory logs, and continues to inspire adoration and sequels.

TWIN PEAKS (1990–1991, ABC) Tracking the investigation into the murder of homecoming queen Laura Palmer in the fictional Washington town of Twin Peaks, David Lynch and Mark Frost's original series basked in surrealism and slowness, and reset expectations of what a television show could be. The titular town's locale is specified by FBI Special Agent Dale Cooper (played by Yakima, Washington–born Kyle MacLachlan) as "five miles south of the Canadian border, and twelve miles west of the state line." This would place Twin Peaks in Washington's northeast corner, but all the Washington settings in the series reside in the western part of the state: the glamorous Great Northern Hotel is the Salish Lodge & Spa in Snoqualmie, Washington (adjacent to the amazing Snoqualmie Falls); the Double R Diner is Twede's Café in North Bend; and Twin Peaks High School is Mount Si High in Snoqualmie, Washington.

TWIN PEAKS: FIRE WALK WITH ME (1992, DIR. DAVID LYNCH) A feature-film prequel to the series, *Fire* depicts the last week in the life of Laura Palmer. Incorporating the garish weirdness of Lynch's Cannes-conquering *Wild at Heart* *and* David Bowie, *Fire* can baffle as an extension of the series, but scores as a searing psychological portrait of an abuse survivor thanks to the brilliant performance of Sheryl Lee as Laura. Added attractions: a new Donna (Lara Flynn Boyle is replaced by Moira Kelly) and a new Twin Peaks High School (Mount Si High is replaced by Snohomish High).

TWIN PEAKS: THE RETURN (2017, SHOWTIME) Twenty-five years after season two, Laura Palmer's murder investigation is reopened. This "limited event series" spreads the story all over the country, but key scenes recur in such familiar locales as Everett (Laura Palmer's house), Snoqualmie (the Fat Trout Trailer Park), and North Bend (the Twin Peaks Sheriff's Department).

PLAIN CLOTHES

(1988 DIR. MARTHA COOLIDGE)

Four years after her charming cult classic *Valley Girl* and four years before her Oscar-nominated drama *Rambling Rose*, director Martha Coolidge made this dumb high-school action-comedy set in Seattle. In *Plain Clothes,* a cop goes undercover as a student to prove his brother's innocence in the fatal stabbing of a teacher at Seattle's Adlai Stevenson High School (portrayed by Ballard's Salmon Bay K-8). Arliss Howard stars as would-be student "Nick Springsteen," Diane Ladd brings the psychodramatic goods to her school-administrator supporting role, and the film's plot and tone flop around confusingly. But it's nice to know that, once upon a time, Ballard played host to Robert Stack, George Wendt, *and* Abe Vigoda (all of whom appear as kooky teachers).

POLICE BEAT

(2005, DIR. ROBINSON DEVOR)

One of the most poetic representations of Seattle on film, *Police Beat* follows an African-born bike cop as he patrols the city. The crimes he finds are alternately garish and mundane, but his countenance remains placid, with his mind perpetually wandering off to thoughts of a complicated romantic relationship. (In the nineties, the film's Zimbabwe-born screenwriter Charles Mudede wrote the "Police Beat" column for the alternative newsweekly the *Stranger*, and the film's crimes are based on real Seattle police reports.) Illuminating our hero's immigrant status is his bifurcated communication: official police interactions are in English, while the narration, which feels like his internal monologue, is in his native West African language Wolof. Leading man Pape Sidy Niang does a beautiful job navigating this dreamlike adventure, which encompasses a whole bunch of visually striking Seattle locales, including the Arboretum, Gasworks Park, the Seattle University reflecting pool, Freeway Park, Dick's Drive-In, and a gorgeous bike ride through Volunteer Park.

POWER
(1986, DIR. SIDNEY LUMET)

Richard Gere stars as a political consultant with a darling mustache and blossoming drama with a public-relations expert played by Denzel Washington, who also has a darling mustache. Regrettably, their mustaches never touch, but the men have an okay time chasing each other around the country during a midterm election year rich with drama and deceit. Only one episode of this episodic political thriller takes place in Seattle, where Gere is called in to help the incumbent governor weather a PR storm, but it features a lovely shot of the legendary building at Denny and Dexter, home to the sweet, standards-blasting KIXI radio and, later, the beloved independent pop station KEXP.

PRACTICAL MAGIC
(1998, DIR. GRIFFIN DUNNE)

Based on the novel by Alice Hoffman, this sister-witch classic stars Sandra Bullock and Nicole Kidman as sibling sorceresses hobbled by a curse that requires any man who loves them to die. Stockard Channing and Dianne Wiest co-star as magic aunts who cheer up the eternal pre-widows with margaritas, and the whole endeavor is awash in a Washington coast lushness that is almost all movie magic (as opposed to actual Washington coast lushness). The witchy aunts' huge Victorian house was built on the San Juan Islands' Friday Harbor—but only the shell of the house was constructed,

continued...

with the inside left hollow and interior scenes shot on a set in California (the Friday Harbor house was torn down after filming). Beyond the stunt house, the scenes of small-town life were filmed in Coupeville, Washington, the historically preserved port town on Whidbey Island, which still celebrates the anniversary of the film's release every year.

RED DAWN
(2012, DIR. DAN BRADLEY)

This remake of the Patrick Swayze-enhanced 1984 action thriller swaps the original's Russians-invade-Colorado plot for a North Korean invasion of Spokane, Washington, where a group of teens take up arms and form a militia to defend their town. Starring Chris Hemsworth and Josh Hutcherson and featuring a crucial appearance by KOMO 4 anchor Dan Lewis, this allegedly Spokane-based film was primarily filmed near Pontiac, Michigan (?!). But at least they managed to pronounce Spokane right.

THE RING
(2002, DIR. GORE VERBINSKI)

A remake so good that many consider it superior to the original, *The Ring* transplants the 1998 Japanese horror film *Ring* to Seattle, which director Verbinski explicitly chose for being "wet and isolated." Naomi Watts stars as a journalist investigating a mysterious videotape that seems to cause the death of anyone who views it, one week after the viewing. Wandering through an increasingly spooky saga starring suicidal horses and soggy waifs, Watts tracks down viewers of the tape, each of whom is a ticking time bomb of impending death, as are we all. Among the featured locales: Seattle's Harbor Steps Apartments, the Port Townsend Ferry Terminal, Deception Pass Bridge, and the Yaquina Head Lighthouse in Newport, Oregon.

SAFETY NOT GUARANTEED

(2012, DIR. COLIN TREVORROW)

In this Sundance hit, sweet-n-sour starlet Aubrey Plaza plays a *Seattle Magazine* intern given a kooky assignment: find and interview the mystery man who placed a classified ad seeking a companion for time travel. The mystery man is played, perhaps unsurprisingly but also very well, by Mark Duplass, who gets to ratchet up his patented normal-guy-doing-stuff goodness with this lethargic sasquatch dream-boy character, who's obviously got a screw loose but is maybe also here to teach us about love and faith and second chances? Plaza's quest for the truth takes her out of Seattle and into the mossy gorgeousness of Ocean Shores, Washington, and in a nice nod to local culture, Duplass's character works at the Grocery Outlet, known colloquially as the "GrossOut."

SAY ANYTHING...

(1989, DIR. CAMERON CROWE)

Say Anything . . . is so many things—the directorial debut of
Cameron Crowe, the source of the eternal "In Your Eyes" boombox
scene, and, according to *Entertainment Weekly*, the best movie
romance of the past quarter-century—that it's almost easy to
overlook that it's a Seattle film.

But from John Cusack's rainy heartbreak drive around Westlake
Center and Wallingford (with The Replacements on the stereo
and *Tapeheads* on the Guild 45th cinema marquee) to Ione Skye's
status as valedictorian at Lakewood
High School, this is a deeply
Seattle movie (that was largely
made in California). The plot
is straightforward: a pair of
seemingly mismatched high
school students (one a
philosophical underachiever,
the other a dutiful
overachiever ready to
break free) fall in love the
summer before the latter
leaves for college. But things
get special fast, thanks in part
to fledgling director Crowe's
deep collaboration with hands-
on producer Polly Platt, whose
genius for unearthing and
maintaining deep idiosyncratic
humanity was showcased in
films like *The Last Picture Show*,
Paper Moon, and *Broadcast*

continued . . .

News, and is put to full use here. (In the film's best non-boombox scene, Cusack's trio of best friends, all female, fuss over the fluctuations of their friend's love life, and it's the sweetest, realest thing you'll ever see.) The supporting characters—John Mahoney's instantly lovable father who's hiding ruinous secrets, Lili Taylor's clear-eyed victim of heartbreak singing revenge folk songs (written by Heart's Nancy Wilson)—are indelible. And the chemistry that powers the film feels real because it is: on the DVD commentary track, John Cusack and Ione Skye speak frankly about falling in (chaste) love with one another during the filming. And while I would love to direct you to the exact Seattle corner where Lloyd Dobler hoisted his boombox, I cannot, because that scene was filmed in Los Angeles, dammit.

SCORCHY

(1976, DIR. HOWARD AVEDIS)

A barely B-movie that delivers an A-plus Seattle-on-film experience (especially if you're high), *Scorchy* stars blonde actress Connie Stevens as a freelance pilot/undercover investigator who poses as an expert in bronze statuary to nab a killer and also swims naked with geese. Shot in a style somewhere between movie-of-the-week and vintage porn, with klutzily dubbed dialogue here and echoey live sound there, *Scorchy* is totally Stevens's show. Awash in hats and headwraps and cross-generational lust, as naked as often as she is bewigged, Stevens attacks this stupid movie like a naked, bewigged pro, and it all culminates in the greatest Seattle chase scene to yet hit celluloid, wherein our heroine leads a pursuer on a multi-vehicle chase that goes on so long and covers so much territory that you will be howling at the screen halfway through. It's an urban ballet of car, motorcycle, taxi, monorail, mini race car, and go-kart that proceeds to a helicopter chasing a speedboat to the San Juan Islands. *Scorchy* is a terrible movie so special that it's earned showcase screenings by the Pacific Northwest's premier purveyors of world-class cinema gawkery, Collide-O-Scope.

SHREDDER ORPHEUS
(1989, DIR. ROBERT MCGINLEY)

Rejected by the Seattle International Film Festival at the time of its release and celebrated with arthouse screenings and an official soundtrack release a decade and a half later, *Shredder Orpheus* is the independent-as-fuck retelling of the Orpheus myth set in a post-apocalyptic wasteland created out of stolen locations and shipping containers, narrated by punk poet Steven "Jesse" Bernstein, with a soundtrack composed by Roland Barker. In 2013, Seattle's Light in the Attic Records released the film's soundtrack on vinyl, packaging it with a DVD of the film.

SINGLES
(1992, DIR. CAMERON CROWE)

Made three years after his solid-gold Seattle rom-com *Say Anything . . .*, Cameron Crowe's poppy, episodic *Singles* follows a group of twenty-somethings as they search for love, sex, and success in grunge-era Seattle.

continued . . .

Kyra Sedgwick and Campbell Scott star as a would-be couple chasing each other through a klutzy courtship, Bridget Fonda co-stars as a self-esteem-deficient barista in love with douchebag rocker Matt Dillon, and members of Pearl Jam appear as Dillon's band Citizen Dick. While some presume *Singles* was designed to capitalize on the Seattle craze engendered by Nirvana's *Nevermind*, the movie hit theaters six days before that climate-changing album was released, and only lucky timing made this sweet, almost sitcom-y film an advertisement for the zeitgeist. It's also a well-stocked time capsule of early-nineties Seattle, home to dance nights at Re-bar, movies at the Neptune, shows at RKCNDY, and Thomas Brothers maps on the floor of your car. For *Singles* superfans hungry for a pilgrimage: the Coryell Court Apartments, where our main characters go about their intersecting lives, resides at 19th Avenue and Thomas Street in Seattle's Capitol Hill neighborhood. Fun fact: although Mayor Tom Skerritt rejects Campbell Scott's idea for a mass-transit system, Seattle would eventually get a light-rail train system in 2003.

SLAVES TO THE UNDERGROUND
(1997, DIR. KRISTINE PETERSON)

In mid-late-nineties Seattle, an all-female grunge band makes noise, fucks boys, assaults rapists, vandalizes porn shops, slides into easy bisexuality, practices tons, and is maybe on the verge of getting a record deal. *Slaves to the Underground* follows all this action up close, with the cast giving performances of spontaneous naturalism and all of it feeling legitimately Seattle-y. To wit: one musician's testimony about a life-changing performance by Ani DiFranco at Bumbershoot.

SLEEPLESS IN SEATTLE
(1993, DIR. NORA EPHRON)

Nora Ephron's starry rom-com stands so tall as a genre-defining blockbuster that re-encountering its humble actuality is a surprise. In *Sleepless*, an eight-year-old imp decides to find his widowed father a new wife. His method: a call-in radio show through which the father's tale of eternal love gone too soon is broadcast nationwide, inspiring a raft of amorous correspondence from America's single women and setting *Sleepless* on its sweet, shaggy path toward love found on top of the Empire State Building.

So what makes this thing so lastingly magical? The stars help. Tom Hanks, who'll spend the years immediately after *Sleepless* collecting Best Actor Oscars for *Philadelphia* and *Forrest Gump*, perfects his patented fractious sweetheart act as a man teetering poignantly between mourning and moving on. Meg Ryan, America's rom-com queen at the height of her reign, brings her fizzy charm and heady intensity to a woman on the verge of having it all, who's harboring an ever-growing feeling that there's something . . . not necessarily more, just *else*. Lording over all is writer/director Nora Ephron, whose wise choices abound, from adhering to a muted color palette and era-generic wardrobe to keep the film visually timeless to engaging the legendary Sven Nykvist—who won international renown and two Oscars for his work with Ingmar Bergman—as cinematographer.

And then there's the setting. Filmed in the late summer of 1992—a season that required producers to fake almost all rain seen on-screen—the movie gives viewers the full Seattle tour, from Pike Place Market (which superfoodie Ephron loved so much she invented a shopping-for-dinner scene to secure its inclusion) to Sea-Tac International Airport, where Hanks's and Ryan's high-stakes eye-meet scene was shot at Gate N7 (and where one can purchase *Sleepless in Seattle* nightshirts in gift shops). Lake Union is home to

continued . . .

TOM HANKS   MEG RYAN

SLEEPLESS
IN SEATTLE

Tom Hanks's incredible houseboat (which sold for over $2 million in 2014), the Athenian at the Market hosts Tom Hanks's and Rob Reiner's beloved tiramisu conversation, and West Seattle's Alki Beach is the destination in a low-speed car/boat chase infamous among locals for its geographical impossibility. ("Throw reality out the window!" says Ephron on the film's commentary track, cementing her rom-com bona fides.) Apart from all the Seattle locales, our city also served as setting for many non-Seattle scenes, with sets for scenes in Baltimore and New York City—including the finale on the observation deck of the Empire State Building!—built in hangars at the decommissioned Sand Point Naval Air Station.

Fun closing fact: the role of the gloriously deadpan babysitter Clarise was played by Seattleite Amanda Maher, who was discovered waiting tables at the legendary health-food restaurant Gravity Bar and hired for what is still her one and only film credit, giving a sharp little performance that inspired Nora Ephron to twice declare her "a genius!" on the film's commentary track.

THE SLENDER THREAD
(1965, DIR. SYDNEY POLLACK)

In future Oscar-winning director Sydney Pollack's debut feature, Oscar winner Sidney Poitier plays a University of Washington student working a suicide prevention hotline, and fellow Oscar winner Anne Bancroft is the voice on the phone, announcing the forthcoming end of her life by her own hand. Such a setup suggests a dry Issue Movie, but what hits the screen is more of a stylish suicide noir, shot in black and white, with a Quincy Jones score and costumes by Edith Head. As Poitier and Bancroft navigate what might be her final hour, the film flashes back to what brought her to this desperate point, with a series of scenes featuring Bancroft wandering around recalling unfortunate moments of her life, pouring out brandy for dead birds, and looking for a reason to live.

continued ...

(Is this film part of the reason Seattle labors under the reputation of "America's suicide capitol?" We're not even in the top ten!) Alongside our leads labor a bunch of other stars (Telly Savalas! Ed Asner! Dabney Coleman!), and the whole thing is a death-scented valentine to Seattle, which is introduced with a stunning aerial shot and rises up recognizably around our characters throughout the film, from Sea-Tac Airport to a rocky waterfront beach to lunch at the Windjammer Restaurant.

SNOW FALLING ON CEDARS
(1999, DIR. SCOTT HICKS)

One of the few films to address the United States' shameful treatment of Asian Americans in the wake of Japan's bombing of Pearl Harbor, *Snow Falling on Cedars* stars Ethan Hawke and Youki Kudoh and tracks a murder case in a tight-knit, racially mixed community in 1950s Washington. Based on David Guterson's beloved novel, the film is set just north of Puget Sound on the fictional San Piedro Island but was filmed on Whidbey Island, in Port Townsend, and in the southern Washington town of Cathlamet on the Columbia River.

Rose Red

(2002, ABC) Written directly for the small screen by horror master Stephen King, *Rose Red* is the miniseries about a haunted mansion and the array of people (residents, parapsychologists) who come to terrible ends inside it. Originally slated to be shot in Los Angeles, the show was relocated to the Pacific Northwest after producers saw Thornewood Castle, a historic Tudor Gothic home in Lakewood, Washington, that in real life is rentable for weddings and on TV became the perfect charming-but-deadly Rose Red Mansion.

SURVIVING THE GAME
(1994, DIR. ERNEST R. DICKERSON)

Ice-T stars as a homeless man hired to guide a group of rich businessmen on a hunting expedition, only to learn that the men's preferred game is . . . Ice-T! A loose, cuss-wordy retelling of the classic story-turned-film *The Most Dangerous Game*, this grim melodrama co-stars F. Murray Abraham, Rutger Hauer, and Gary Busey as the hunting party (who occasionally call each other "faggot motherfuckers") and all boils down to an Ice-T versus F. Murray Abraham forest death battle, all shot in and around Lake Wenatchee and Okanogan-Wenatchee National Forest.

THIN SKIN
(2020 DIR. CHARLES MUDEDE)

Directed by Charles Mudede (the screenwriter behind *ZOO* and *Police Beat*) and featuring a script co-written by Mudede, *Shrill* creator Lindy West, and star Ahamefule Oluo, *Thin Skin* follows a Seattle jazz musician as he feels his way through an extravagant season of upheaval, including divorce, the sudden appearance of estranged family, and one big medical mystery. In between the plot-forwarding scenes come musical interludes, with our trumpeter protagonist and a small jazz combo communicating in music what he can't in words. Based on Oluo's hit stage show *Now I'm Fine*, the film was shot entirely in Seattle, from Jefferson Park to downtown's Owl 'n Thistle pub to North Seattle College.

PNW Film All-Stars

From Hepburn to Streep to Poitier, big-ass stars, have been drawn to PNW cinema so regularly they've earned de facto citizenship.

JEFF BRIDGES: In the late eighties/early nineties, the versatile Hollywood mainstay starred in three Seattle-based films that saw him hit career peaks and veer into weirdness. In *The Fabulous Baker Boys* (page 33), he's a gifted asshole with an ambivalent crush on Michelle Pfeiffer; in *American Heart* (page 8), he's an ex-con rebuilding his life in Pioneer Square; and in *The Vanishing* (page 81), he's a creepy Norwegian with dark secrets and a brain-bending accent.

MARK DUPLASS: When not writing, directing, and producing films with his brother, Jay, Mark Duplass spent the late aughts/early 2010s as the go-to leading man for Seattle-based independent film, lending his idiosyncratic charm to 2009's *True Adolescents* (page 77) and *Humpday* (page 45), 2011's *Your Sister's Sister* (page 45), and 2012's *Safety Not Guaranteed* (page 63).

JULIANNE MOORE: Before ascending to Oscar-winning stardom, Moore was a supporting player who improved any movie she entered, including four PNW-ers. In *The Hand That Rocks the Cradle* (page 41), Moore's spirited ex-girlfriend charms all before learning a terrible lesson about greenhouses; in *Assassins* (page 9), she has a secret life as a computer hacker and also has a cat; in *Benny & Joon* (page 14), she's Aidan Quinn's hash-slinging love interest; and in *Body of Evidence* (page 98), she's a betrayed wife who gets to slap Madonna.

RIVER PHOENIX: Cinema lost much when this exceptionally talented film actor died, but a trio of Northwest movies capture what he had to offer from all sides: the soul-deadening complexities of childhood in *Stand by Me* (page 135); the softness under the tough surface of a military recruit in *Dogfight* (page 29); and the existential restlessness of a narcoleptic street hustler in *My Own Private Idaho* (page 95).

KEANU REEVES: Cinema's most soulful mannequin has starred in one crucial PNW film (two, if you count *Point Break,* page 127) and provided noteworthy support in two others. Best in show: Reeves's dilettante rent boy delivering fake Shakespeare in *My Own Private Idaho* (page 95). Runners-up: his outrageous pantomime of Siddhartha in *Little Buddha* (page 51) and his spiritually hungry orthodontist in *Thumbsucker* (page 138).

ALLY SHEEDY: *The Breakfast Club*'s sullenest teen has a resume dotted with PNW film roles, including Gene Hackman's overshadowed daughter in *Twice in a Lifetime* (page 78), Matthew Broderick's charming girlbud in *WarGames* (page 83), and the grating female lead in the awful *Short Circuit* (page 134).

THIS BOY'S LIFE
(1993, DIR. MICHAEL CATON-JONES)

Based on the classic memoir by Tobias Wolff, this coming-of-age drama stars Ellen Barkin and Leonardo DiCaprio as a mother and son who relocate to 1950s Seattle for a better life, only to encounter Robert De Niro's flat-topped, performatively upstanding suitor, who woos Barkin and abuses DiCaprio. In Wolff's memoir, the brutal facts of the plot are perpetually offset by the brilliance of the prose—every sentence drives home that the kid getting clobbered not only survived but thrived. But there's no such comforting artistry to the film, which can feel like a one-note boxing match between hammy De Niro and the convincingly brutalized DiCaprio. The vast majority of this cinematic brutality goes down in Concrete, Washington, the upper Skagit Valley logging town where De Niro moves with Barkin and DiCaprio. For the film, Concrete was given a 1950s makeover so elaborate that town leaders considered having the financially struggling Concrete go forward as a 1950s time-capsule tourist destination. But it turns out not many people feel the need to visit the place where Robert De Niro beat the shit out of Leonardo DiCaprio. Live and learn.

TROUBLE IN MIND
(1985, DIR. ALAN RUDOLPH)

One of the most distinctive Seattle films, Alan Rudolph's *Trouble in Mind* takes place in a future that looks like the 1940s, where a collection of noir types—a coffee-shop queen, a just-sprung ex-con, a struggling young father seeking business opportunities (legal or not), various gangsters—intersect in an urban police state called Rain City, which looks exactly like Seattle. (It should: *Trouble in Mind* was filmed entirely on location, from the new-wave sex party at the Camlin Hotel to the Seattle Monorail, which

is presented as Rain City's primary mode of transportation.)
More significant than plot development is the movie's stagey
dreamscape feel, seemingly emanating from the gathered works
of film noir sprinkled with LSD. Kris Kristofferson stars as the ex-
con protagonist, Geneviève Bujold is the wise diner owner, Keith
Carradine's the family-man-turned-hophead criminal, and an out-
of-drag Divine provides crucial support as the mafia boss Hilly Blue,
whose home mansion is played by the Seattle Asian Art Museum.
(There's a house party scene!) "Here is a movie that takes place
within our memories of the movies," wrote Roger Ebert in his four-
star review, and he's right. But it also totally takes place in Seattle,
and the city should be proud.

TRUE ADOLESCENTS
(2009, DIR. CRAIG JOHNSON)

Mumblecore Mastroianni Mark Duplass stars as a stagnating thirty-
something musician who pays the bills postering street poles and
winds up moving in with his aunt (Melissa Leo, two years before
her Oscar win). Tasked with chaperoning his nephew's camping
trip, Duplass is called into something like responsible adulthood,
with iffy results. (Yes, he keeps the kids alive, but he also makes
them listen to the Sonics while holding forth on the brilliance of
the Sonics.) Found-moment films like this one live or die by the
pace of the revelations, and True Adolescents could be a little
speedier. Still, there are plenty of Seattle totems, including the
Comet Tavern, some Rainier tall boys, a Mariners name-check, and
a sullen Mark Duplass in a knit hat, sadly eating a granola bar.

TUGBOAT ANNIE
(1933, DIR. MERVYN LEROY)

The first major motion picture to be shot in Seattle, *Tugboat Annie* is the tale of a sweet-n-salty female tugboat skipper wrangling family dramas and various tugboat-related challenges in the fictional Puget Sound town of Secoma, Washington. It was also a total effing blockbuster, starring the beloved duo Wallace Beery and Marie Dressler (the Oscar-winning latter of which appeared on the cover of *Time* just after the film's release) and earning over $1 million at the box office to become MGM's most profitable film of 1933. To be fair, the majority of the movie was shot on Culver City soundstages, but Seattle was the movie's spiritual home, with local residents (including Seattle's then-mayor John F. Dore) appearing as extras. The titular character's beloved tugboat remains in Seattle's Northwest Seaport.

TWICE IN A LIFETIME
(1985, DIR. BUD YORKIN)

This star-packed slice-of-life drama stars Gene Hackman as a married Seattle steelworker whose midlife attraction to another woman inspires him to leave his stable, loving family for a new adventure. Ellen Burstyn is brilliant as the jilted wife who warms to her new freedom, Ann-Margret plays the abashed but willing homewrecker, and Amy Madigan earned an Oscar nomination as the daughter who takes the divorce exceptionally hard. It all goes down in Holden, Washington, a fictional suburb of Seattle portrayed by the city of Snohomish, and the whole film's awash in Puget Sound culture, from Seahawks and Mariners talk among off-duty steelworkers to hilly streets so steep the sidewalks have footholds cut into them. Hackman's beloved blue-collar bar the

Shamrock Tavern is actually the Dubliner in Seattle's Fremont neighborhood, and his first divorced-dad apartment is a perfectly shrimpy sad thing on Capitol Hill (that he's thrilled to have, just like real life!). Bonus: the movie's title song is written and performed by Paul McCartney.

TWILIGHT
(2008, DIR. CATHERINE HARDWICKE)

A primer in codependency and risky intimacy, the *Twilight* saga follows moody teen Bella Swan as she moves to a small town on the Olympic Peninsula and becomes entangled with attractive and deadly vampires. Besides teaching a generation of high schoolers and horny receptionists about the thrills and drawbacks of hot vampire love, *Twilight* made an international hotspot of Forks, Washington, where the movie is famously set but not actually filmed—that would be Oregon, primarily, with the Swan house in the city of St. Helens, the Cullen home in Portland, and the Forks Diner in Damascus. Still, Washington State provided locales for some crucial scenes, such as Bella and Edward's forest-flying fiesta (shot on the Washington side of Columbia River Gorge) as well their first official date, shot at Port Angeles's Bella Italia, where Bella's first-date meal—Olympic forest-mushroom ravioli in creamy besciamella—is forever on the menu. And Forks, Washington, is absolutely the center of the real-world Twilight Industrial Complex, hosting the annual "Forever Twilight in Forks" festival every September. Here fans can stay at Twilight Lodgings (home to cabins used in the sequels *Eclipse* and *Breaking Dawn*), enroll in "Cook Like Bella" classes, cosplay like mad, and visit the permanent exhibit of *Twilight* props and costumes at the Rainforest Arts Center.

Twilight

UNFORGETTABLE

(1996, DIR. JOHN DAHL)

Filmmaker John Dahl made a name for himself with the taut, stripped-down neo-noirs *The Last Seduction* and *Red Rock West*, then used his clout to make this un-taut, overwrought, would-be thriller with a plot so convoluted that several American film critics died attempting recaps. The gist: Ray Liotta is a medical examiner in a very dark and rainy Seattle, where he's taking an experimental drug meant to help him retrieve the memories of murder victims, in hopes that such info will help nab killers or something. "In the annals of cinematic goofiness, *Unforgettable* deserves a place of honor," wrote the venerable Roger Ebert. "This is one of the most convoluted, preposterous movies I've seen." Shot primarily in British Columbia, *Unforgettable* features some nice local establishing shots, plus a scene where Liotta's character points out Garfield High School (his alma mater) from the observation deck of the Space Needle.

THE VANISHING

(1993, DIR. GEORGE SLUIZER)

In 1988, Dutch filmmaker George Sluizer released *The Vanishing*, a slow-burn thriller tracking one man's hunt for his missing girlfriend, which built to one of the most powerful and unnerving endings in cinema. In 1993, Sluizer was hired by Hollywood to remake his film for English-speaking audiences, rebooting the story in the Pacific Northwest with Kiefer Sutherland and Sandra Bullock as the splintered couple and Jeff Bridges as the sociopath who methodically turns their lives upside down. The resulting film was seemingly focus-grouped to death, ultimately being named "the worst remake of all time" by *Salon*'s Matt Zoller Seitz.

continued . . .

While the remake's addition of such mainstream Hollywood tropes as a heartwarming love interest and justice for victims drew derision from fans of the original, such changes might be perfectly okay with new viewers who aren't aware that the first *Vanishing* doesn't end with a triumphant escape. They might even like the new version (especially if they appreciate goofy love subplots and fatal shovel stabbings). Whatever the case, *The Vanishing*'s US remake is rich with PNW vibes, from Jeff Bridges' Ballard-scented kook (complete with Swedish accent) to Sutherland and Bullock's Volvo station wagon topped with a loaded bike rack. Featured locations include the Seattle Yacht Club, Sur La Table in Pike Place Market, and the Mountainside Shell Station in North Bend, Washington (where the titular vanishing takes place).

WAITING FOR THE LIGHT

(1990, DIR. CHRISTOPHER MONGER)

One of the kookiest Hollywood movies ever situated in the PNW, *Waiting for the Light* is an early-sixties period piece starring Teri Garr as a single mother who moves to Washington to raise her kids and run a diner. Shirley MacLaine co-stars as the family's eccentric Aunt Zena, a former vaudeville magician who tags along to Washington, where she stages a trick that convinces their new neighbors and eventually the rest of the nation of an angelic presence come to deliver humanity from the Cuban Missile Crisis. The movie's offbeat Washington town was constructed out of scenes filmed in the cities of Buckley, Puyallup, Seattle, and Tacoma.

WARGAMES

(1983, DIR. JOHN BADHAM)

A teenage computer whiz (presciently located in a Seattle suburb) accidentally engages the secret supercomputer that controls the United States' nuclear arsenal. Believing he's playing a game, he blithely triggers the countdown to World War III, instigating a global governmental freakout and a tense-as-fuck race to fix the earth-endangering mistake. Matthew Broderick stars as our teen hacker, Ally Sheedy plays his sparkly eyed best friend, Dabney Coleman dabs out as a Department of Defense dude, and screenwriters Lawrence Lasker and Walter F. Parkes were nominated for an Oscar for their highly effective script. Partly shot in Washington State, the film used new sets (the NORAD headquarters set was built in the Cascades!) and repurposed locales (the Oregon airport was really Boeing Field).

WHERE'D YOU GO, BERNADETTE

(2019, DIR. RICHARD LINKLATER)

In Seattle-based writer Maria Semple's thoroughly Seattle-y novel *Where'd You Go, Bernadette*, a middle-aged woman in Seattle is mentally paralyzed by her past achievements, locked in a cold war with passive-aggressive neighbors, and estranged from her life as a wife and mother—so she up and disappears. Richard Linklater's cinema adaptation stars Cate Blanchett as the title character, Kristen Wiig as her nemesis neighbor, and, for the most part, Pittsburgh and Vancouver, BC, as Seattle. But there are plenty of respectful Seattle establishing shots, the Koolhaas-designed downtown library is basically a supporting character, and there are some very Seattle-y plot points (a Microsoft product launch, precipitation that eventually pulls a hill down onto a house).

WORLD'S GREATEST DAD

(2009, DIR. BOBCAT GOLDTHWAIT)

This pitch-black comedy stars Robin Williams as a fledgling writer and single father of a seriously troubled teen. When his son abruptly dies, Dad can't resist exploiting the loss to forward his writing career, instigating a cavalcade of deeply immoral behavior. Shot in Seattle, the film makes good use of a couple local landmarks, including Wallingford's McDonald International Elementary (which plays the film's high school) and Nirvana's Krist Novoselic, who has a wordless cameo. Fun fact: while filming in Seattle, Robin Williams did a surprise drop-in set at the Laff-Hole comedy night at Re-bar!

SEATTLE VÉRITÉ

Along with supplying setting and acting as muse, Seattle has served filmmakers as a subject, inspiring a number of world-class documentaries.

STREETWISE (1984, DIR. MARTIN BELL) In this essential Seattle documentary, a film crew haunts the de facto sex-and-drug exchange east of Pike Place Market, getting close with the teenage drug dealers and sex workers hustling on the streets of what had recently been crowned "America's most livable city." It's harrowing, with scene after scene of kids navigating the darkest adult concerns and emerging with the hardness that only perpetual survivors possess. But it's also roiling with life, as these gun-toting, drug-smoking, queer-bashing kids seize their days—meeting with social workers,  visiting estranged parents, dyeing their hair in gas-station bathrooms, jumping off bridges into Puget Sound. Give it your full attention, and you'll never forget it. (In 2016, *Streetwise* birthed a sequel, *Tiny: The Life of Erin Blackwell*, illuminating the adult life of one of *Streetwise*'s most memorable kids. Both are available in the Criterion Collection.)

EAST OF OCCIDENTAL (1986, DIR. MARIA GARGIULO) For twenty-eight minutes that pack a punch, *East of Occidental* blends archival photos with contemporary interviews to tell the story of Seattle's International District, where immigrants from China, Japan, and the Philippines—united by nothing but crude Caucasian perception—created a still-thriving world of art, commerce, and vast family life west of 12th and Jackson. From immigration bans and quotas to internment camps, the denizens of the International District have withstood endless avalanches of bullshit and have the self-possession (and often towering wryness) to prove it. This short, sharp doc captures it all to powerful effect. (Available on the streaming service Kanopy.)

HYPE! (1996, DIR. DOUG PRAY) *Hype!* is two great documentaries in one. The first charts the "Northwest music scene" in all its dumb, noisy, dorky brilliance, with the *Hype!* team producing state-of-the-art live shows to capture a slew of local bands at their best. The quality of this live footage earned filmmakers the trust of the local scene, which came to understand that this wouldn't be just another TV documentary about Nirvana and grunge.

Which brings us to *Hype!*'s second great documentary subject: the industry-upending explosion that met Nirvana's *Nevermind*, a Michael Jackson–toppling surprise blockbuster, which inspired a lunatic gold rush to "find the next Nirvana" and wring every possible dollar from the grunge jackpot. The international hype avalanche is meticulously represented, with jaw-dropping montages of "grunge pencils," baggy flannel on the runway, and former Sub Pop receptionist/current Sub Pop CEO Megan Jasper's legendary Lexicon of Grunge, a collection of made-up phrases ("swingin' on the flippity flop") pulled from her butt and printed in the *New York Times*. Outside the hype, Nirvana is warmly treated like just another great Northwest band, here represented by the first-ever public performance of "Smells Like Teen Spirit," captured on VHS at Seattle's OK Hotel.

Besides delivering killer live performances, TAD, Fastbacks, Screaming Trees, Soundgarden, Gas Huffer, 7 Year Bitch, Mudhoney, and others sit for interviews, showing off the goofy chemistry and friendship that fueled so many of the bands. That this ramshackle, half-a-joke but totally ass-kicking music scene produced art that made the world go bonkers is both perfectly fitting and a hilarious fluke, and *Hype!* shows exactly why.

THE HEART OF THE GAME (2005, DIR. WARD SERRILL) At Seattle's Roosevelt High School, new coach Bill Resler is hired to take the girls' basketball team from very good to state-conqueringly great. This engrossing doc follows Resler and the Roosevelt Roughriders for six seasons, with the on-court thrills (Roosevelt versus Garfield, forever) punctuated with serious sociological drama. Narrated by Ludacris!

Hype!

ZOO (2007, DIR. ROBINSON DEVOR) The essayistic *ZOO* explores the community around an Enumclaw farm where animal-loving men from around the country gather to get fucked by horses. After a man dies from injuries sustained in a stable, *ZOO* becomes a rural legal drama as authorities scramble to hold someone criminally responsible—only to learn that Washington State lacks a law criminalizing interspecies sex. Can animals consent? What if the animal's the top? And how long does it take to draft and pass a law outlawing horse fucking? These are the questions of *ZOO*, and it's all as weird and spooky and gawkworthy as it sounds.

I AM SECRETLY AN IMPORTANT MAN (2010, DIR. PETER SILLEN) In the late seventies and throughout the eighties, Seattle performance poet Steven "Jesse" Bernstein came on like a one-man punk band armed with text instead of songs and earned opening spots for artists from William S. Burroughs to Big Black. *I Am Secretly an Important Man* memorializes the poet through a wealth of video footage while charting the chaotic forces that went into creating him. It doesn't end well, but it's a thrill (and sometimes a shock) getting there.

PORTLAND & OREGON

Look for a unifying aesthetic of Oregon cinema and you'll be lost. Like Interstate 5 winding from the sparse and woodsy southern Willamette Valley up to the dense and bridge-loving Portland, the cinema of Oregon covers dramatically different terrains. A distinguishing characteristic is innovation, with Oregon playing home to artistic breakthroughs from the golden age of silent films (Murnau's *Sunrise*, Buster Keaton's *The General*) to today's most gawkworthy stop-motion animation (the oeuvre of LAIKA Studios). Oregon soil has nurtured both singular cinema auteurs (Gus Van Sant, Kelly Reichardt) and ordinary folk whose lives are worthy of cinematic attention (*Alien Boy*'s James Chasse, everyone who appears in *How to Die in Oregon*).

There are recurring themes. The Oregon wilderness has inspired decades of stories of pioneers and other off-the-grid types, the earlier of which sang, danced, and bought wives (*Seven Brides for Seven Brothers*, *Paint Your Wagon*), the latter of which mostly just hung around hoping to avoid notice (*Old Joy, Leave No Trace*). Oregon cinema is also seriously in love with literature, with adaptations of books powering so much Oregon cinema, from bestselling classics (*The Black Stallion, Sometimes a Great Notion*) to the contemporaneous book-to-movie pipeline that's continually flowing for Kelly Reichardt and Gus Van Sant.

What follows is not exhaustive, but is alphabetical. If you notice a classic Oregon movie missing, it's likely because of the shooting-location switcheroo, wherein a seemingly obvious Oregon movie—*I, Tonya; A League of Their Own*—was actually filmed somewhere else.

Test for ignorant interlopers, onscreen and off: the pronunciation of the state name, which, in the mouths of posers, becomes Or-uh-GONE. (Here's looking at you, Richard Benjamin in *How to Beat the High Cost of Living*.)

Jack Nicholson

Oregon has no greater cinematic avatar than Jack Nicholson, the Jersey-born Hollywood legend who's created iconic characters in a trio of classic Oregon-based films. In the existential family drama/road pic *Five Easy Pieces* (1970, dir. Bob Rafelson), Nicholson roams disaffectedly around Oregon and Washington (including the legendary scene in a Eugene Denny's). His fledgling screen persona blooms before our eyes, with Nicholson's ability to ride a mood while showing up for distinct, intense scenes earning him a Best Actor Oscar nomination. Five years later, he'll take home the prize for *One Flew Over the Cuckoo's Nest*, Miloš Forman's 1975 adaptation of the novel by Oregon literary hero Ken Kesey, in which Nicholson's patented Jack act finds a rich, heartbreaking new context in the Oregon State Hospital. Finally, there's *The Shining*, Stanley Kubrick's 1980 adaptation of Stephen King's novel, starring Nicholson as off-season property manager driven mad by time, space, and ghosts, and featuring northern Oregon's Timberline Lodge as the beautiful and doomed Overlook Hotel. (Exterior only—the Overlook's interior was inspired by Colorado's Stanley Hotel, with interior scenes shot almost entirely on soundstages in England. Movies!)

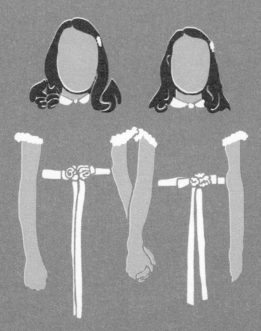

A.I. ARTIFICIAL INTELLIGENCE
(2001, DIR. STEVEN SPIELBERG)

Steven Spielberg's inherited-from-Kubrick sci-fi chiller follows a state-of-the-art mechanical boy from his life as an emotional doula for a grieving suburban mom to his flight into the tech-strewn wilderness. It's a brainy, chilly, high-tech reboot of Pinocchio, and one of its crucial scenes takes place in Oregon. When he is no longer wanted by his suburban family, mechanical-humanoid boy Haley Joel Osment is driven by his mother/purchaser—in a futuristic car that looks like a Volkswagen-brand Roomba—through the foothills of Oxbow Regional Park in the Sandy River Gorge, en route to his desertion in the woods.

ALIEN BOY: THE LIFE AND DEATH OF JAMES CHASSE
(2013, DIR. BRIAN LINDSTROM)

A Portland punk-scene denizen so distinctive he inspired a song by the Wipers, James Chasse spent his post-punk years living in downtown Portland, conversing with friends about art in the Powell's café, and navigating an occasionally debilitating mental illness. In 2006, in broad daylight in front of a dozen eyewitnesses, Chasse was violently apprehended and beaten by three police officers, which left him with injuries that proved fatal. This documentary gets deep into the Chasse family's "excessive force" lawsuit against the City of Portland. It's a wrenching procession of still-shocked eyewitnesses, cops squirming on the stand, and no spoilers here.

ANIMAL HOUSE

(1978, DIR. JOHN LANDIS)

A blast of anti-authority snottiness on par with *Never Mind the Bollocks, Here's the Sex Pistols*, *National Lampoon's Animal House* is the blockbuster comedy chronicling the war between an in-your-face fraternity of misfits and the upstanding dean of fictional Faber College. Set in 1962, it's a traditional morals-bashing cavalcade of hand jobs, food fights, gross racism, impersonations of popped zits, and performances so good—by Peter Riegert, Tom Hulce, Donald Sutherland, Karen Allen, and exploding star John Belushi—it somehow adds up to something substantial. Providing crucial support: the University of Oregon in Eugene, which welcomed filmmakers with open arms; University President William Beaty Boyd even permitted filmmakers to use his office as the fictional Dean Wormer's. Other locales: the Dr. A. W. Patterson House in Eugene stood in for the misfit heroes' Delta House, and the final parade scene was filmed on Main Street in Cottage Grove.

BENJI THE HUNTED

(1987, DIR. JOE CAMP)

In the fourth film in the Benji series, everyone's favorite li'l scruff pup is on location filming a movie (meta!) when he becomes lost at sea and washes up in the wilderness of Oregon—with four orphaned cougar kittens! I should probably stop using exclamation points now because *Benji the Hunted* abruptly shifts from adventure romp to harrowing blood sport, as the hunter who made those cougar kittens orphans continues to stalk the woods loaded for Benji. (Everything turns out okay; this is a kid-friendly franchise.) Among the Oregon filming locales: Newport, Astoria, and Young River Falls.

GUS VAN SANT

Gus Van Sant's career encompasses everything from Oscar-anointed studio projects (*Good Will Hunting, Milk*) to innovative art films (*My Own Private Idaho, Elephant*). He's also a Portland resident who's made a slew of films set in Portland and the Pacific Northwest.

MALA NOCHE (1988) "I wanna show this Mexican kid that I'm gay for him." So drawls our protagonist Walt, a lackadaisical convenience store clerk who spends the whole of *Mala Noche* approaching his goal from a variety of amoral angles. The kid in question is a non-English-speaking immigrant, whom Walt plies with food, drink, and money, all done so placidly it could count as courting. With its masterful weaving of images and spoken text, and plainspoken, non-political homosexuality, the black-and-white *Mala Noche* (made on a $20,000 budget) remains one of Van Sant's most powerful works. It's also one of his most Portland-y, from its source material (the autobiographical novella by Portland writer Walt Curtis) to its spontaneously found locations around Old Town in NW Portland.

DRUGSTORE COWBOY (1989) Van Sant's critical breakthrough stars Matt Dillon and Kelly Lynch as Portland dope fiends who maintain their habit by robbing drug stores. Based on the autobiographical novel by James Fogle, the movie's a grim, darkly funny diary of shared addiction and the divergent paths people take to move on. Winner of the National Society of Film Critics' awards for Best Film and Best Director, the film makes good use of Portland's Pearl District, with key scenes going down at The Pharmacy in Nob Hill and the (old) Ace Hotel.

MY OWN PRIVATE IDAHO (1991) A New Queer Cinema classic, Van Sant's eagerly inventive, Shakespeare-scented tale stars River Phoenix and Keanu Reeves as rent boys hunting for love and family on the streets of Portland and Seattle. It's a fearless, too ambitious queer mélange, capturing the career-best performance by Madras, Oregon, native River Phoenix as well as a wealth of iconic PNW locales. In Portland, there's The Governor Hotel, Washington Park, and the Video Follies adult store. (The Chinese restaurant where the hustler friends congregate is now

continued . . .

Bailey's Tap Room on SW Broadway.) In Seattle, there's the Gatewood Hotel, the St. Regis Hotel, and, for serious PNW historians, a name-check of the bizarre Northwest-Mexi health food chain Macheezmo Mouse. (The Idaho road scenes—including the falling-house orgasm—were shot near Maupin, Oregon.)

ELEPHANT (2003) Based in part on the student massacre at Columbine High, *Elephant* tracks the events surrounding a suburban school shooting—which sounds dreadful, but Van Sant's revelatory tweaking of the timeline and deep facility with young actors make it something special, one of his most powerful movies and winner of Best Film and Best Director at the 2003 Cannes Film Festival. *Elephant* was filmed on the campus of Portland's Whiteaker Middle School (before it was demolished for its dangerous levels of mold and rayon gas).

PARANOID PARK (2007) Another small, intense kid-based project, *Paranoid Park* chronicles a teenage skateboarder who lands in the middle of an accidental killing and its attendant police investigation. Based on the book by Portland-based novelist Blake Nelson, the movie has a dreamscape feel with elliptical but sharply drawn home lives for the core characters and naturalistic acting from the largely non-professional cast. Among the filming locations: Burnside Skatepark, Lloyd Center, Portland State University, Madison High School, and Van Sant's personal beach house.

DON'T WORRY, HE WON'T GET FAR ON FOOT (2018) After a drunken car crash made him a quadriplegic at age twenty-one, Portland's John Callahan gave up booze and took up cartooning, with his shockingly hilarious one-panels appearing in the *Willamette Week* newspaper for twenty-seven years. Van Sant brings this singular Portland story to the screen with a star-packed cast (Joaquin Phoenix, Jonah Hill, Jack Black) and a real good performance from Beth Ditto of beloved Portland band Gossip. Filmed primarily in California, the movie features scenes at Powell's City of Books, Portland State University, and in the Wasco County city The Dalles.

My Own Private Idaho

THE BLACK STALLION

(1979, DIR. CARROLL BALLARD)

Another kids' movie set in Oregon featuring an animal-endangering shipwreck (see: *Benji the Hunted*), *The Black Stallion* brings the 1941 children's novel to serious cinematic life. After the harrowing capsizing of a boat comes a twenty-eight-minute stretch of wordless action, as the two shipwrecked inhabitants of an island off the coast of Africa—a young boy and a fiery stallion—come to know their surroundings and each other. Once rescued and shipped to America, they proceed into the film's second half, wherein the boy learns to ride his new best friend with help from Mickey Rooney. Among the Oregon locales: the oceanside town of Gearhart, the bayside town of Nehalem, and the Liberty Theater in Astoria.

BODY OF EVIDENCE

(1993 DIR. ULI EDEL)

The cinematic component of Madonna's three-pronged 1992–1993 fuckblitz (also featuring the softcore *Sex* book and the great *Erotica* album), *Body of Evidence* stars our queen as the BDSM-fluent lover of a rich old man who dies while doing it, leaving Madonna with a murder charge and a creepy, BDSM-curious lawyer played by Willem Dafoe. The Meryl Streep of lip-synching, Madonna remains unconvincing as a dialogue-delivering actor, forever betrayed by her diffuse focus and "Am I doing this right?" delivery. Also, like Rick James's "Super Freak" boast of "incense, wine, and candles," the alleged shocks *Body of Evidence* offers are more provincial than creators seem to know. But that's what makes it so fun to point and laugh at, and the whole thing's very Portland-y: Madonna's killer copulation goes down at Pittock Mansion, her character is said to have once been

continued . . .

a resident at Mount Hood Substance Abuse Center, and after being charged with murder-fucking, she's bailed out of Multnomah County Jail.

But wait, there's more! *Body of Evidence*'s crucial courtroom scenes were filmed not in Portland but in Olympia, Washington, where Madonna's presence in the marble-paneled

senate chamber at the State Capitol Building caused a commotion. "The plot is that the character played by Madonna seduces a man to death," fumed Washington Secretary of State Ralph Munro in a letter of complaint to the Department of General Administration. "Why should we condone or cater to anything of this kind?" A spokesperson for the department replied straight to the *Los Angeles Times*: "We are not a censoring agency," said Christine Yorozu to the *Times'* Jane Galbraith. "We feel that since Madonna's got all of her clothes on in the courtroom scenes, the use of the facility is totally appropriate for us."

C.O.G.
(2013, DIR. KYLE PATRICK ALVAREZ)

Based on a short story by David Sedaris, C.O.G. follows David (Jonathan Groff), a recent Yale graduate who feeds his hunger to connect with the real world by taking a job at an Oregon apple orchard. Here he intersects with an array of oddballs, most of 'em sweet, cult-y Christians with dark underbellies, but there's a gay would-be rapist thrown in too. Over a Steve Reich soundtrack, amid the beauty of an orchard in autumn, things get weird and C.O.G. becomes a psychological drama with religious underpinnings, all of it filmed on location in Forest Grove, Oregon.

DEAD MAN
(1995, DIR. JIM JARMUSCH)

Jim Jarmusch's obtuse acid trip of a Western sets a pretty, pre-Disney Johnny Depp loose on the late-1800s western frontier, where he shoots a man, befriends an aboriginal mystic, and engages in stiff, showily theatrical interactions with Billy Bob Thornton, Iggy Pop, Crispin Glover, John Hurt, and Robert

Mitchum. Stylized out the wazoo and too static by half, the film boasts an alternately spooky and clangy score by Neil Young, as well as (non-subtitled) conversations in the Cree and Blackfoot languages, plus tons of beautifully shot PNW locales, including Oregon's Grants Pass and Applegate River, and Washington's Neah Bay and Columbia River Gorge.

DANCING ON THE TECHNICOLOR FRONTIER!

Asked to characterize Oregon's cinema aesthetic,
contemporary viewers would likely draw examples from
the "people wandering around quietly in the woods" genre
exemplified by *Captain Fantastic, Leave No Trace*, and the
work of Kelly Reichardt and later Gus Van Sant. But once upon a
time, Oregon was where people came to bust a fucking move.
Exploding with color and (more often than not) big song-and-
dance numbers, Oregon's frontier epics are among American
cinema's weirdest and most ravishing offerings.

SEVEN BRIDES FOR SEVEN BROTHERS (1954, DIR. STANLEY
DONEN) Nominated for Best Picture at the 1955 Academy Awards
(where it lost to *On the Waterfront*), this CinemaScope hootenanny
set in 1850s Oregon concerns seven brotherly backwoodsmen who,
um, physically persuade a corresponding number of townswomen
to come live with them as wives. It's a sexist horror, with woman
after woman traded "like she was a bag of meal . . . to slave for
slummocky backwoodsmen!" But there are also dazzling dance
numbers, choreographed by Michael Kidd, which transform prosaic
frontier tasks (barn raising, chopping wood) into large-scale dance
extravaganzas. There is also a scene of erotic cow milking. Stupidly,
this classic Oregon adventure was not filmed in Oregon, but
on MGM sound stages. Nevertheless, Oregon is such a primary
character in the story that the whole film gets grandfathered in.
Supplementary fact: *7B47B* served as inspiration for *Here Come
the Brides,* the late-sixties/early-seventies television series that
transplanted the imported-wife action to nineteenth-century
Seattle, with opening credits set to Hugo Montenegro's eternal
blue-sky jam "Seattle."

HOW THE WEST WAS WON (1962, DIRS. JOHN FORD, HENRY HATHAWAY, AND GEORGE MARSHALL) Nominated for Best Picture at the 1963 Academy Awards (where it lost to *Lawrence of Arabia*), this epic in five chapters follows a westward-expanding family over a run of historically rich decades in the nineteenth century, covering everything from the gold rush and the Civil War to the construction of the railroads. Starring a buttload of marquee names including John Wayne, Debbie Reynolds, Henry Fonda, and Gregory Peck, the film required the work of three fully grown directors, all of whom were required to navigate the demands of Cinerama, the widescreen process that called for scenes to be triple shot with three different cameras and screened via three projectors. (*West* is one of only two fiction films ever made in the format.) Tragically, *How the West Was Won* features zero singing and dancing, but there is a scene where a lady pushes James Stewart down a well. Among the film's Oregon locales: the sweeping natural vistas of Eugene and Grants Pass.

PAINT YOUR WAGON (1969, DIR. JOSHUA LOGAN) Nominated for nothing at the Academy Awards, this Paddy Chayefsky–scripted film adaptation of the 1951 Lerner and Loewe musical stars Lee Marvin and Clint Eastwood as scheming adventurers in the California gold country. Here they buy and share a wife, successfully campaign to legalize prostitution, and transform a mining camp into a boomtown. Also, both men sing. The results are a weird failure that killed the humungo musical trend sparked by *The Sound of Music* and almost works as camp. And while your author never wants to see *Paint Your Wagon* again, he would pay good money to Kickstart a documentary about the making of the film, which involved constructing a budget-devouring, gold-rush-era mining camp in northeast Oregon's Wallowa-Whitman National Forest, where cast and crew slept in on-location tents amid dwindling food and film supplies.

THE FISHERMAN'S BRIDE
(1909, DIR. FRANCIS BOGGS)

The first film with a plot ever made in Oregon, the silent short *The Fisherman's Bride* is a twisty story of love amid Astoria fisheries, filmed at the mouth of the Columbia River. "A story founded on facts, as old Skipper Stout and his daughter Jennie live near Astoria, Oregon," summarized the *East Oregonian* in 1909.

FOXFIRE
(1996, DIR. ANNETTE HAYWOOD-CARTER)

Based on the Joyce Carol Oates novel *Foxfire: Confessions of a Girl Gang*, this tough and pulpy teen drama concerns a quartet of high-school girls who gather around an iconoclastic new student. Before long, this fledgling girl gang is exacting revenge on a handsy male teacher, with their intoxicating new power and freedom taking them to the edge. Starring a pre-superstardom Angelina Jolie, a pre–Rilo Kiley Jenny Lewis, and certified Don Juanita Jenny Shimizu (the actor and model who famously dated Madonna, Ione Skye, and Angelina Jolie), the film was shot in Portland, with scenes at Burnside Skatepark, Lincoln High School, and, in one terrifying segment, on the Broadway Bridge.

FREE WILLY
(1993, DIR. SIMON WINCER)

This heartwarming family-friendly hit concerns a killer whale that's about to be executed by immoral aquarium owners and the headstrong Portland boy who fights to save him. Together these species-discordant misfits fight the power, find their purpose, and forge a friendship that will last until Willy leaps over the kid to ocean freedom. Starring Keiko the whale in a stereotypical role (will we never get to see him in a period drama?) and co-starring

continued . . .

Free Willy

Lori Petty and Michael Madsen as the Willy-whispering boy's foster parents, *Free Willy* inspired two sequels, a television series, and a direct-to-video reboot. It also inspired the rehabilitation and release of the formerly captive Keiko, whose transition to freedom did not go well. Reintroduced into the ocean off Iceland, Keiko failed to integrate and eventually died of pneumonia. (Sorry. If you need cheering up, watch *The Goonies*.) Along with a ton of Portland locales—including Burnside Skatepark, Hawthorne Bridge, and Tom McCall Waterfront Park—the film makes use of Warrenton and Hammond Marinas, where filmmakers shot the magical-leap finale. Bonus: former Astoria mayor Willis Van Dusen makes a cameo appearance as a fish vendor!

THE GENERAL

(1926, DIRS. CLYDE BRUCKMAN AND BUSTER KEATON)

In this Buster Keaton classic, Keaton's stone-faced engineer must save his girl and his train amid the chaos of the Civil War. To shoot the film, Keaton headed for Lane County, Oregon, home to the narrow-gauge railroad tracks capable of accommodating the film's antique locomotives. Setting up camp in the town of Cottage

continued...

Grove, the cast and crew (along with their spouses and kids) created a little working village that was warmly welcomed by the locals, including five hundred members of the Oregon National Guard who played the Union and Confederate armies. Cottage Grove is also where producers constructed the bridge over Rock River, which, once cameras were rolling, they set on fire, sending an actual locomotive onto the burning bridge and causing both bridge and train to collapse into the river below. The $42,000 scene was the most expensive of the silent film era, and in 2007, *The General* placed eighteenth on the American Film Institute's list of the Greatest Movies of All Time.

THE GOONIES
(1985, DIR. RICHARD DONNER)

As fun as a roller coaster and twice as screamy, this kid-thrilling cult classic concerns the residents of the "Goon Docks" neighborhood of Astoria, where tough financial times are pushing blue-collar parents toward foreclosure and inspiring the neighborhood's kids to solve everyone's problems by hunting down the long-lost treasure of a seventeenth-century pirate. Sean Astin, Corey Feldman, Martha Plimpton, and Josh Brolin star as adventuring kids; Anne Ramsey leads the crime family determined to claim the treasure first; and it all plays out with comic-book precision in a world rich in adolescent shock humor designed to be quoted on middle-school playgrounds. (Also, in the grand tradition of eighties kid flicks, the girl characters suck, with *The Goonies'* girls presented as hysterical scolds incapable of doing anything. On the other hand, there is the glory of Sloth.) Filmed all over Astoria, with scenes at Columbia Memorial Hospital and the old Clatsop

continued . . .

WILD WILD COUNTRY

(2018, DIRS. CHAPMAN WAY AND MACLAIN WAY) This hit Netflix documentary series casts a splashy spotlight on Rajneeshpuram, the religious community that built a utopian city deep in Wasco County, Oregon, in the 1980s, until bioterror attacks and political assassination attempts brought the whole murderous sex cult toppling down. It's a well-documented freak show, led by Rajneesh's diabolically charming first mate Sheela, who easily earns the Best Supporting Actress in a Documentary Oscar that continues to not exist.

County Jail (now home to the Oregon Film Museum). City-sponsored anniversary events have drawn over 10,000 *Goonies* fans to Astoria, with the house that served as the Walsh family home drawing so many visitors that the city eventually limited public access.

HEAR NO EVIL
(1993, DIR. ROBERT GREENWALD)

Six years after her Best Actress Oscar win for *Children of a Lesser God*, Marlee Matlin stars as a deaf Portland woman whose life is upended by a corrupt stalker cop who believes she's hiding a valuable coin he desires and torments her in all sorts of deafness-exploiting ways. Brought to the screen by the man who directed *Xanadu*, *Hear No Evil* features zero mystical roller skating and a lot of increasingly intense ASL interrogations and sadistically brutal killings. In the best scene, John C. McGinley rocks out to reggae while driving across Portland's Hawthorne Bridge and learns a terrible lesson. Other Portland locales: Union Station, the Veterans Memorial Coliseum, Washington Park's International Rose Test Garden, and Manor House at Lewis & Clark College. Beyond PDX: the climax finale was shot at the Timberline Lodge at Mount Hood.

HEAVEN ADORES YOU

(2014, DIR. NICKOLAS DYLAN ROSSI)

Born in Nebraska and raised in Texas, singer/songwriter Elliott Smith found his calling in Portland, making a small racket with his band Heatmiser before whispering his way to stardom as a solo artist. This loving documentary does a particularly good job capturing the deep connection that Portland music lovers and music makers had to Smith and his work, from eyewitness testimony of shockingly intimate early gigs to friends still stunned by his sudden and mysterious death in 2003.

HOW TO BEAT THE HIGH COST OF LIVING

(1980, DIR. ROBERT SCHEERER)

In 1980 America, inflation is Enemy #1, with soaring gas and grocery prices sending middle- and lower-class families into situational poverty. In this fizzy comedy, a trio of Eugene, Oregon, housewives (portrayed by Jane Curtin, Susan Saint James, and future Oscar-winner Jessica Lange) fight back by planning a million-dollar heist at the local mall (Eugene's Valley River Center, right next to the Willamette River, which is a crucial character in the heist). A sort of suburban 9 to 5 with a Porky's sensibility, the movie is adolescently salacious—Jane Curtin's character escapes two perilous situations via impromptu sex work played for laughs—but it's also stupid fun and seriously star-packed, with the female leads supported by Dabney Coleman, Richard Benjamin, and Fred Willard.

Shrill

(2019–2021, HULU) Based on Lindy West's 2016 book of autobiographical essays, *Shrill* is the Hulu comedy series following Portland writer Annie as she navigates sex, love, and ambition in a world still too ready to see her only as fat. *Saturday Night Live*'s Aidy Bryant stars and is brilliant as Annie, John Cameron Mitchell exerts himself to great effect as Annie's narcissistic boss at *The Weekly Thorn* newspaper, and all three seasons are filled with unique delights, from raw dog nights and morning-after pills to fat femme pool parties and no-big-whoop abortion. Filmed all over Portland and surrounding Oregon, with standout scenes on the coast at Manzanita, the Coleman Guest Ranch in Molalla, and downtown Portland's Oaks Amusement Park.

HOW TO DIE IN OREGON

(2011, DIR. PETER RICHARDSON)

In 1997, Oregon enacted its Death with Dignity Act, which permits terminally ill residents to end their lives with doctor-prescribed medication. In this bracing documentary, a number of Oregonians dealing with end-of-life issues share their stories with the camera, holding forth on life and death and medicine in ways that will shock you and expand your mind.

I DON'T FEEL AT HOME IN THIS WORLD ANYMORE

(2017, DIR. MACON BLAIR)

This Sundance-conquering lowkey indie thriller concerns a depressed Portland woman who responds to a home burglary by joining forces with her weird but devoted neighbor to deliver vigilante justice. They soon find themselves in a world of scary thrills, broken fingers, and criminality way out of their depth. Starring the always-great Melanie Lynskey alongside a mossy Elijah Wood, the film was filmed all over Portland and won the Grand Jury Prize for the US Dramatic competition at Sundance 2017.

INTO THE WILD

(2007, DIR. SEAN PENN)

Based on Jon Krakauer's bestselling nonfiction book, *Into the Wild* concerns a most promising young man who leaves college loaded with disillusionment and soon finds himself alone in the Alaskan wilderness eating poisonous plants until he is dead. Emile Hirsch stars as our doomed hero who writes a farewell note to the world before his corpse is found by moose hunters. In a weird production twist, scenes set in Atlanta were instead filmed in Portland and surrounding Oregon, with our protagonist's graduation from Atlanta's Emory University filmed at southeast Portland's Reed College, and the post-graduation lunch enjoyed by Hirsch, Marcia Gay Harden, and William Hurt held at McCormick's Fish House in Beaverton.

KINDERGARTEN COP
(1990, DIR. IVAN REITMAN)

In between *Total Recall* and *Terminator 2,* Arnold Schwarzenegger starred in this comedy directed by Ivan *"Ghostbusters"* Reitman, in which an Arnold Schwarzenegger–shaped police investigator must go undercover as a kindergarten teacher. Here he comedically clashes with toddlers while solving

crime, finding love, and unearthing his latent passion for teaching. Co-starring PNW theater favorite Pamela Reed as Arnold's police officer sidekick (whose stature as a friend-not-love interest is communicated by her always eating humongous sandwiches), *Kindergarten Cop* makes great use of Astoria, from John Jacob Astor Elementary School (where many students and faculty played extras in the film) to the Bayview Motel and Commercial Street. (The school picnic was shot at Ecola State Park near the city of Cannon Beach.)

THE LAST BLOCKBUSTER
(2020, DIR. TAYLOR MORDEN)

A sweet, slight documentary about the video store chain that devoured the Friday nights of a generation, *The Last Blockbuster* travels to Bend, Oregon, to profile the nation's last remaining Blockbuster store as it prepares for its at-long-last closing. Produced by Netflix, it's flimsy stuff, overloaded with nostalgia from say-nothing talking heads, perfect for ignoring while you do stuff on your phone.

LEAN ON PETE
(2017, DIR. ANDREW HAIGH)

In this visually stark, emotionally rich adaptation of the novel by Portland-based author Willy Vlautin, a teenager with a rough home life escapes into his job working for a horse trainer, befriending an old racehorse, which he takes on a heartbreaking journey through gorgeously stark Oregon terrain. Directed by Andrew Haigh, the British filmmaker behind 2011's gay mumblecore romance *Weekend*, *Lean on Pete* stars Charlie Plummer, Chloë Sevigny, and Steve Buscemi as inhabitants of this odd and shifty world where people are still basically trying to do their best, whatever they believe that to be. As Sevigny's character tells our kid protagonist, in hopes of sparing him some hurt: "He's not a pet, he's just a horse." Filmed in Oregon, including scenes at Portland Meadows racetrack and the Dabney State Recreation Area in the town of Corbett.

LEAVE NO TRACE

(2018, DIR. DEBRA GRANIK)

Deep in the vast Forest Park near Portland, a military-vet dad and his thirteen-year-old daughter have built a relatively harmonious off-the-grid life that's entirely contingent on staying hidden. When a simple mistake busts their secrecy, they flee the woods for county-funded shelter and medical attention, exposing the daughter to such exotic niceties as refrigerators, casseroles, and 4-H Club, and spotlighting the generational rift that will fuel the rest of the story. Based on the novel *My Abandonment* by Portland author Peter Rock and starring Ben Foster and Thomasin McKenzie, *Leave No Trace* bypasses the political posturing and relative melodrama of the similarly plotted *Captain Fantastic* for a you-are-there docudrama feel and up-close humanity. Among the Oregon locales: Portland's St. Johns Bridge, Aerial Tram, and VA hospital, and Estacada's Serenity Mountain Retreat, aka the oldest nudist club west of the Mississippi, which served as the film's non-nudist shelter camp.

LOST HORIZON

(1973, DIR. CHARLES JARROTT)

This musical production of the *Lost Horizon* story—first told in James Hilton's 1933 novel, then Frank Capra's 1937 film—finds its star-packed cast surviving a Himalayan plane crash to recuperate in the magical valley lushness of Shangri-La. Here they engage in vast pageantry while performing long, slow, heavily art-directed musical segments built around songs by Burt Bacharach and Hal David, and hailed by Roger Ebert in the *Chicago Sun-Times* as "the most incompetent and clumsy dance numbers I've ever seen." The most widely ridiculed movie in the PNW cinema canon, *Lost Horizon* was something of the *Showgirls* of its day—an endlessly hyped,

continued...

LAIKA Studios

Just outside of Portland in Hillsboro, Oregon, in a 140,000-square-foot, state-of-the-art soundstage, a small universe of artists constructs vast, intricate worlds out of tangible materials. These worlds and their constructed inhabitants are then photographed frame by frame, creating stop-motion animation films that have literally all been nominated for Academy Awards. Growing out of Will Vinton's Vinton Studios (creators of the California Raisins and coiners of the term Claymation), LAIKA Studios burst onto the feature-film scene with 2009's *Coraline*, an adaptation of Neil Gaiman's book about a gothy girl and her spooky mirror world, created via LAIKA's pioneering use of 3D printing. The Oscar-nominated offerings continued with 2012's *ParaNorman*, 2014's *The Boxtrolls*, 2016's *Kubo and the Two Strings*, and 2019's *Missing Link*.

big-budget flop that became a name-checkable touchstone of failure, with virtually everyone in the public square driven to take a swing. (Best in show: Bette Midler, who delivered the indelible "I never miss a Liv Ullman musical!") In addition to the ill-used Ullman, the cast features Peter Finch, Sally Kellerman, George Kennedy, Michael York, Charles Boyer, and John Gielgud, and the Himalayas are co-played by Washington's Cascade Mountains and Oregon's Mount Hood. Mostly shot on Hollywood soundstages, the movie also filmed at the Timberline Lodge in Mount Hood, Oregon, and at Lake Chelan, Washington. (Also, don't take the *Showgirls* comparison too literally. *Showgirls* is ten bad movies trying to kill each other and never, ever boring, while *Lost Horizon* is, unfortunately, boring as zzzzz.)

MEN OF HONOR
(2000, DIR. GEORGE TILLMAN JR.)

Cuba Gooding Jr. stars in the true story of the first African American US Navy diver along with the bewigged Robert De Niro who trained him. Made with the endorsement of the Navy, the film plays out like an old man's sentimental, self-aggrandizing memories, and while it's heartening to watch Gooding break through the Navy's racial barriers, it involves a whole bunch of N-bombs plus terrible acting from De Niro. There are also a handful of scenes shot at PNW locales, including the towns of North Plains and Dibblee Point in Oregon, as well as Longview, Washington.

THE REAL WORLD:
PORTLAND

(2013, MTV) For the reality-TV juggernaut's twenty-eighth season, the requisite seven strangers were corralled in Portland in a two-story building at 9th Ave and NW Flanders St. When not working at Cool Harry's yogurt shop or boning in the bathroom of Pizza Schmizza Pub & Grub, the cast went snowboarding on Mount Hood, sightseeing at Bridal Veil Falls, and fishing at the Columbia River Gorge. But the season's most memorable moment occurred in cast member Nia's vagina, into which she'd inserted a kegel toning device, which she was then unable to retrieve. Spoiler alert: it eventually emerged, with the cast celebrating the birth of the device they'd named Eggbert. In a poor reflection of Portland's respect for history, Eggbert's birthplace remains unmarked by plaque or statue.

MAVERICK
(1994, DIR. RICHARD DONNER)

Based on the late-fifties/early-sixties TV series starring James Garner, *Maverick* stars Mel Gibson as a playboy riverboat gambler, Jodie Foster as his conniving love interest, and a returning James Garner as the lawman out to get 'em. Primarily shot in Utah, Arizona, and California, the movie also makes good use of the Pacific Northwest, where filmmakers sent the last remaining sternwheel tugboat in the US—named *The Portland* and housed at the Oregon Maritime Museum—down the Columbia River.

MR. BROOKS

(2007, DIR. BRUCE A. EVANS)

Sentient Oroweat loaf Kevin Costner stars as a wealthy businessman who moonlights as a serial killer with the help of his evil alter-ego who looks exactly like William Hurt. Dane Cook and Demi Moore co-star, as a fledgling killer obsessed with Costner and the gum-chewing investigator out to nab him, respectively. It all goes down in a very rainy Portland that is actually mostly Shreveport, Louisiana, except for one scene shot on-location at Portland's Cup & Saucer Cafe.

PORTLANDIA

(2011–2018, IFC) Spoofing Portland's stature as lefty utopia while dabbling in all-purpose daffiness, *Portlandia* made new types of stars of creators Fred Armisen and Carrie Brownstein and cemented Portland's reputation as an artisanal lifestyle mecca. Over its eight seasons on IFC, the show built a world of overlapping characters, many of them played by notable guest stars. (Kyle MacLachlan's Mayor of Portland has an assistant played by Sam Adams, former mayor of Portland.) And of course, the show was filmed all over town: the feminist bookstore Women and Women First was played by the feminist bookstore In Other Words, the "Fart Patio" sketch was shot at the vegan café Prasad, and the series-launching "Dream of the '90s" video was filmed at the Vera Katz Eastbank Esplanade along the Willamette River.

MR. HOLLAND'S OPUS
(1995, DIR. STEPHEN HEREK)

Richard Dreyfuss stars in this decade-spanning drama about a would-be composer who sidelines his professional art ambitions for a thirty-year career as a public-school music teacher and reliable suburban father. Olympia Dukakis co-stars as a spiky principal with a heart of gold, William H. Macy scowls at rock 'n' roll from under a buzzcut, and the timeline's thirty-year span is driven home through numerous montages. *Mr. Holland's Opus* fucking loves montages and isn't fussy about making them good. In one, footage of Vietnam and the moon landing plays over John Lennon's "Imagine." If you like having your tears jerked, *Mr. Holland's Opus* will give you a happy ending. Filmed in and around Portland, including Ulysses S. Grant High School and the University of Portland.

OVERBOARD
(1987, DIR. GARRY MARSHALL)

Overboard is the comedy about an amnesia-ridden heiress who falls in love with the widowed single dad who kidnaps and enslaves her. Goldie Hawn stars as the heiress-turned-housewife, and Hawn's real-life partner, Kurt Russell, co-stars as the single father who convinces Hawn's kidnapped amnesiac that she is his wife and brings her home in the bed of his truck. Kurt's kids play along, calling her Mom to her face and saying, "She might have no tits, but she has a nice ass" behind her back. (However creepy, Hawn's "nice ass" appears in numerous scenes, in various bathing suits and body stockings, and, in fact, gives Miranda July's celebrated ass in *The Future* a run for its butt.) *Overboard* is a cartoonish affair, with hoary plot points and long-winded, heavily scripted insults for our sparring romantic leads who sometimes seem like they're doing

continued...

community theater. But underneath it all is a core of pain found in Goldie Hawn's character, a woman who is rejected and exploited by everyone she knows. Her actual husband refuses to recognize her. Everyone's trying to get rid of her, to pawn her off on someone else, and when this former tantrum-throwing show-bitch learns to love what's in front of her while operating a profitable mini-golfery, it's a beautiful thing.

Ostentatiously set in Oregon—with radios announcing, "Oregon, good morning!"—*Overboard* was largely shot in California. The movie also fails the state pronunciation test, going full "Or-uh-GONE." Nevertheless, the birthday party scene was filmed in Newport, Oregon, and there's official Portland Trail Blazers merch all over. One of the most fertile creative properties of modern times, *Overboard* has been adapted into film remakes in four countries, TV shows in two countries, and is currently airing in its original form on at least three cable channels as you read this.

PAY IT FORWARD
(2000, DIR. MIMI LEDER)

In suburban Las Vegas, a twelve-year-old boy launches a goodwill movement known as "pay it forward," a sort of humanitarian spin on the pay-for-the-next-car's-Starbucks gag that makes for good Instagram but ruins baristas' lives. Haley Joel Osment stars as the good Samaritan boy, Helen Hunt and Kevin Spacey co-star as Osment's alcoholic mother and creepy social studies teacher (guess who's who!), and the bulk of the movie's scenes were shot in Las Vegas and Los Angeles. However, a crucial late scene was filmed in Portland, where a down-on-his-luck drug addict pays it forward by talking a woman out of throwing herself off St. Johns Bridge.

PIG
(2021, DIR. MICHAEL SARNOSKI)

Continuing his singularly weird and totally awesome late-career trajectory, Nicolas Cage stars as a mumbly deep-woods truffle hunter with a rich backstory and a beloved foraging pig. After his titular pig is kidnapped, our grubby hero must venture out of the Oregon wilderness and into Portland's black-market foodie scene. The mossy deep-green woods of the opening segments have an almost gothic Grimm Brothers feel, and the pig is fucking adorable, with so much character in its eyes that it forges an instant connection with the camera and audience, and frankly makes Babe look like a pile of shit. Among the Portland locales: the Helen Bernhard Bakery, the sandwichery NoPoBoys, and the Saucebox restaurant.

Grimm

(2011–2017, NBC) In this modern-day expansion of the Brothers Grimm cinematic universe, a Portland homicide detective accepts his ancestral calling as a supernatural-creature hunter tasked with maintaining the earthly balance between humans and mythological beasts. The whole run of the show was shot on location in Portland, which show creators described as "the ideal setting for fairy tales," thanks to the vast forestry areas of both Washington Park and Forest Park. Bonus: the show's supernatural creatures are named things like Blutbad, Zauberbeist, Jägerbar, and Dickfellig.

POINT BREAK

(1991, DIR. KATHRYN BIGELOW)

Seventeen years before her Best Director Oscar for *The Hurt Locker*, Kathryn Bigelow directed this deeply dumb action classic starring Patrick Swayze as a bank-robbing surfer mystic and Keanu Reeves as the undercover FBI agent tasked with bringing him down (without falling under his spell!). Filmed primarily in southern California, *Point Break* also makes strategic use of Oregon, with the rainy Australian outpost that draws Swayze and Reeves portrayed by the south-of-Astoria town of Wheeler, and the devouring-ocean finale shot at Indian Beach in Ecola State Park, just outside Cannon Beach, Oregon. Fun fact: *Point Break Live!*, an audience-interactive stage adaptation of the Bigelow film, debuted at the Northwest Film Forum in Seattle in 2003, becoming a national sensation with productions in Las Vegas, Chicago, and Los Angeles, with the show running at various locations around Hollywood and LA for nine years.

PREFONTAINE

(1997, DIR. STEVE JAMES)

Born and raised in Coos Bay, Oregon, Steve Prefontaine is the long-distance-running Olympian so awesome he earned dueling biopics. The first and best Prefontaine pic—shot in an engrossing documentary style by Steve James (co-creator of the beyond-engrossing documentary *Hoop Dreams*)—stars eventual Oscar winner Jared Leto as the weird, prickly, not-super-likeable running sensation who won adoring fans through accomplishment alone. R. Lee Ermey co-stars as Coach Bill Bowerman, and Lindsay Crouse, the cocky broad with the flat affect from *House of Games* (page 46), plays Pre's German-born mom. The whole cast adheres to the documentary-scaled performances, even when things get seriously dramatic at the Munich Olympics. Alongside the triumphs, the

continued...

film captures the threadbare, sometimes crushingly uncertain day-to-day existence of even superhero sports figures. Weirdly, this Oregon story was filmed primarily in Washington: in Tacoma, the University of Puget Sound's Peyton Field was reconfigured to resemble the University of Oregon's Hayward Field, and in Seattle, Fremont's Buckaroo Tavern served as the Coos Bay bar where Pre's friends and local fans watched his Olympic competitions. And then there is *Without Limits* (1998, dir. Robert Towne). Directed by the legendary screenwriter of *Chinatown, Shampoo,* and *The Last Detail, Without Limits* stars a perfectly good Billy Crudup as Prefontaine, a creepy Donald Sutherland as Coach Bowerman, and a lady who sounds like Count Chocula ("You vant my boy to go to University of Oregon?!") as Pre's mom. The dialogue's clunky, the tone is sappy, but at least this crucial Oregon story was shot in Oregon, using the University of Oregon's actual Hayward Field and Bill Bowerman's actual house.

THE PUNK SINGER

(2013, DIR. SINI ANDERSON)

In the opening scene of Sini Anderson's vivid documentary of artist/activist/foundational riot grrrl Kathleen Hanna, a young Hanna is seen on a small stage in Olympia delivering a sharp, stinging spoken-word piece. Soon after, Hanna reports in contemporary voiceover, she met the postmodernist writer Kathy Acker, who advised our fledgling slam poet that if she wanted to be heard, she should form a band. Hanna took her advice, and the epochal Bikini Kill was born. *The Punk Singer* tracks Hanna from her teen years in the PNW—where her family moved when she

continued . . .

Prefontaine

KELLY REICHARDT

The films of Portland-based filmmaker Kelly Reichardt have been described by the director herself as "just glimpses of people passing through"—a technically appropriate description that undersells the richness of the worlds Reichardt creates. Known for slow, quiet films that often focus on rural working-class characters, Reichardt made her feature film debut with 1994's Florida-based *River of Grass*, then got to making a number of films set and shot in Oregon.

OLD JOY (2006) Starring actor Daniel London, singer/songwriter Will Oldham, and hardly anyone else, this adaptation of a story by Portland-based writer Jonathan Raymond follows what the author calls "competitively compassionate male friends," as they reconnect while camping in Mount Hood National Forest. The people are only part of the story, with Reichardt and cinematographer Peter Sillen spending as much time and focus on surrounding nature as interpersonal dynamics. Words are few, takes are long, and it's all lightly meditative—a style Reichardt will hone in her coming films.

WENDY AND LUCY (2008) Michelle Williams stars as a young woman en route to a cannery job in Alaska when her traveling-companion dog goes missing in a small Oregon town. What plays out on screen is essentially a lost-dog procedural as we follow Williams's Wendy on her hunt for dog Lucy. There's no backstory, just practical, problem-solving forward motion, adding up to a slice of life so real you'll wish the crew would drop the cameras and help. It's a riveting movie about a life constricted by arbitrary policies no one takes responsibility for, but at least they're nice about it sometimes. Filmed in Portland and Wilsonville, Oregon.

MEEK'S CUTOFF (2010) Reichardt and Michelle Williams rejoin forces for this minimalist western set in mid-1800s Oregon, where a group of settlers crossing the Oregon high desert find themselves mired in a trip of extended duration and dwindling supplies. The brutal facts of trail realities spool out slowly and prosaically, but there are also arrestingly poetic sequences—a near-dance of women crossing a river on foot, a settler chasing a wind-blown scarf across cracked earth. Filmed in the Cascade Mountains and Harney County, Oregon, and featuring a name-check of the Willamette Valley (pronounced correctly).

NIGHT MOVES (2013) Armed with stars and the meatiest plot of her career, Reichardt applies her visually rich/verbally thrifty style to a slow-burn tale of eco-terrorism in the Pacific Northwest. Jesse Eisenberg, Dakota Fanning, and Peter Sarsgaard star as three strangers brought together to execute an attack on the Green Peter Dam in Linn County, Oregon. This we watch them do in precise detail—acquiring nitrogen from a farm-goods supplier, navigating a speedboat to the hit point. But in *Night Moves*'s second half, shit gets real, as these criminally intimate strangers fight to cover their tracks without turning on each other. Shot on location in southern Oregon, including scenes at Chief Miwaleta County Park in Azalea, Oregon, and the Galesville Reservoir (playing the Green Peter Dam) in the Klamath Mountains.

FIRST COW (2019) In 1820s Oregon, a chef traveling with a band of fur trappers befriends a Chinese immigrant on the run for killing a man. Together they forge a conspiratorial food-based friendship. Eventually the pair's closeness and their curious foodstuffs draw attention, unleashing horror and building to a mercifully elliptical ending. Reichardt's most accomplished work, *First Cow* was named Best Film at the 2020 New York Film Critics Circle Awards.

THE SIMPSONS

(1989–FOREVER, FOX) Now in its thirty-third season, the most important comedy of its generation (and a reasonably okay entertainment vehicle for generations after) has deep PNW roots. Show creator Matt Groening was born in Portland and attended the Evergreen State College in Olympia, Washington, but the most delightful showcase for Simpsonalia is the collection of Portland streets bearing names that eventually turned up as cartoons, including Flanders, Kearney, Lovejoy, Quimby, Terwilliger (and some count Burnside).

was fourteen, and where her young art life bloomed in Olympia and Portland—through her twenty-first-century chapters in NYC where she married a Beastie Boy, battled an insidious illness, and continued making singular art with her bands Le Tigre and The Julie Ruin.

RING OF FIRE

(1961, DIR. ANDREW L. STONE)

In this pulpy juvenile-delinquent eco-drama, a group of horny, jazz-talking toughs and their fast-girl queen kidnap a cop, whom they sexually harass until one of their cigarettes starts a forest fire, and then it's all "Help me, Daddy-O!" Filmed in Wynoochee River, Washington, and Vernonia, Oregon, this dumb movie features footage from two actual forest fires!

THE RIVER WILD
(1994, DIR. CURTIS HANSON)

Meryl Streep goes action hero as a rafting-expert mom battling murderous Kevin Bacon on a raging river. Filmed primarily on white-water rivers in Montana, *The River Wild* features additional scenes shot on the Rogue River north of Medford, so rejoice, Oregonians, your waters have indeed been graced by Queen Streep.

ROARING TIMBER
(1937, DIR. PHIL ROSEN)

In this log-based romantic thriller, the toughest logger in Oregon logging country contends with deadlines and competitors who seek to foil his logging while simultaneously wooing a young logging heiress. Starring silent-to-sound crossover star Jack Holt and a whole bunch of Astoria, Oregon.

ROOSTER COGBURN
(1975, DIR. STUART MILLAR)

One year after tearing up Seattle streets in *McQ*, John Wayne returns to the Pacific Northwest as another rogue cop busted for brutalizing suspects, this time in late-nineteenth-century Oregon. *Rooster Cogburn* finds Wayne reprising his Oscar-winning role from the 1969 film *True Grit*, as the ornery one-eyed US Marshal Reuben J. "Rooster" Cogburn, who here ventures to earn back his badge by capturing a posse of bank robbers. Joining him is Katharine Hepburn, a seventy-something spinster stalwartly searching for her father's killer. Shot entirely in Oregon, the film makes picturesque use of the mountains west of Bend, the whitewater rapids of the Deschutes River, and the Smith Rock State Park northeast of Redmond.

SHORT CIRCUIT

(1986, DIR. JOHN BADHAM)

What if E.T. and R2-D2 had a charmless baby that rocked out to DeBarge while dodging the wrath of the US military? This is the elevator pitch for *Short Circuit*, in which a robot designed to walk bombs into Moscow is struck by lightning and gains super-robot powers, including human curiosity, awesome dancing, and an instant facility with eighties slang. Adopted by animal caregiver Ally Sheedy while being hunted by good-hearted government employee Steve Guttenberg, our robot engages in endless cutesy behaviors and also watches *Saturday Night Fever* (directed by the same man who directed *Short Circuit*!). All of this happens in Astoria, Oregon (where Sheedy lives and is quirky), and at the Bonneville Dam in the Columbia River Gorge (on the Washington side, where the fictional, robot-creating Nova Laboratories is located).

No-fun fact: Fisher Stevens dons brownface and Apu-mouth to play Steve Gutenberg's East Indian sidekick, which Stevens later explicitly regretted in an interview with *The Trouble with Apu* writer/director Hari Kondabolu.

SOMETIMES A GREAT NOTION
(1971, DIR. PAUL NEWMAN)

Based on the novel by Ken Kesey and directed by and starring Paul Newman, this shaggy family drama concerns a contentious Oregon clan fighting to keep their logging business alive while warring with logging rivals who also happen to be neighbors. Co-starring Henry Fonda and Lee Remick and set in a big, old waterfront house in the fictional community of Wakonda (!), the movie tackles the return of a prodigal son, a multi-family football game turned fistfight fueled by Olympia beer, and a whole bunch of logging, a dull activity overshadowed by the ever-present threat of deadly violence. Filmed along the Oregon Coast and featuring Kernville, Yaquina Bay, the Yaquina River, and the city of Newport, the movie ends with an exciting log transport set to twangy Mancini music, featuring a severed arm holding up a middle finger.

STAND BY ME
(1986, DIR. ROB REINER)

The best movies about kids foreground the fact that childhood can be hell. Based on Stephen King's 1982 novella and set in 1959 Oregon, *Stand by Me* concerns a quartet of boys slogging through thoroughly grim lives, who together make a trek to see a boy's dead body near some distant train tracks. Physically beaten and emotionally starved by their caretakers, with even their weekend escape centered around a friend's corpse, and besieged by cruel teen bullies, the boys—played by Wil Wheaton, River Phoenix, Corey Feldman, and Jerry O'Connell—nevertheless find their pleasures in jokes and stories, and a camaraderie that can devolve into shit-talk but coalesces instantly around a shared threat. The film's grimness is offset by seriously gratifying bully comeuppance

continued...

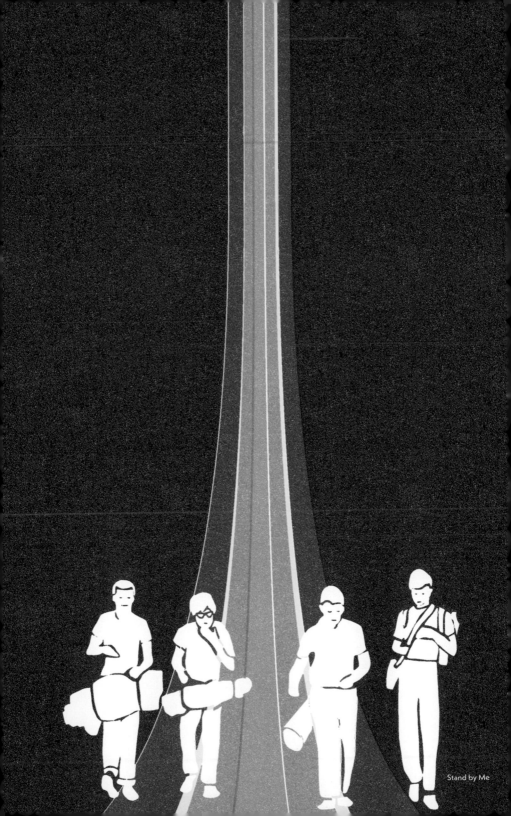

Stand by Me

and a memorable segment concerning a pie-eating contest at a county fair. The film's fictional town of Castle Rock was played by the real town of Brownsville, Oregon, which has held an annual "Stand by Me Day" since 2007, and has embedded a penny in the street right where Jerry O'Connell's Vern found one in the film.

SUNRISE
(1927, DIR. F. W. MURNAU)

From the director of 1922's *Nosferatu* comes this silent fable of a husband, a wife, and the temptations that almost ruin them. Subtitled "A Song of Two Humans," it's a shocking, emotionally riveting story of betrayal and forgiveness, with its most indelible scenes taking place on the banks and in the water of Oregon's Columbia River. Winner of Best Picture (Unique and Artistic Production) at the 1929 Academy Awards, *Sunrise* was named the fifth best film of all time in the British Film Institute's 2012 critics' poll.

SWORDFISH
(2001, DIR. DOMINIC SENA)

In this awful action thriller, John Travolta is an ex-con computer hacker with an international reputation and a noticeable wig, Hugh Jackman is an up-and-coming computer ninja who successfully executes a hacking while receiving a blowjob at gunpoint, and Halle Berry is the beautiful queen of the heist crew, until she is hanged by her neck from a crane and fatally shot. (There is also a ludicrously gratuitous topless scene.) The script is a cliché parade, with everyone tossing out adolescent zingers and no one making fun of Travolta's wig. But the (admittedly exciting) opening aerial sequence featuring Travolta and Sam Shepard was shot on location in Bend, Oregon, with additional footage shot in the Oregon towns of Smith Rock and Terrebonne.

THUMBSUCKER
(2005, DIR. MIKE MILLS)

In this quirkily stylized dramedy, a high-school boy in the fictional town of Beaverwood, Oregon, struggles to overcome his thumb-sucking with the help of orthodontic witchery and a Ritalin prescription. Tilda Swinton stars as the boy's great weird mother (a rehab nurse with a secret life and a celebrity obsession), Keanu Reeves co-stars as the mystical orthodontist, and it was 99.9 percent shot in Oregon, from Trillium Lake in Clackamas County to Tualatin High School in Tualatin, Oregon.

WHAT THE BLEEP DO WE KNOW!?
(2004, DIRS. WILLIAM ARNTZ, BETSY CHASSE, AND MARK VICENTE)

Easily the dumbest movie earning mention in this book (sorry, McQ!) *What the Bleep* is a hybrid documentary featuring iffy ramblings on quantum physics interspersed with a fictional story starring Marlee Matlin as a spiritual seeker with a head full of questions. A collection of stoner thoughts presented with the patina of science, the movie makes good use of beautiful, misty Portland (mostly the Goose Hollow neighborhood). Fun fact: co-director/co-writer Mark Vicente was a member and then an outspoken critic of the multilevel marketing company and criminal cult NXIVM!

WILD
(2014, DIR. JEAN-MARC VALLÉE)

Cheryl Strayed's 2012 memoir *Wild* found the author processing her exploded life by hiking a thousand miles alone along the Pacific Crest Trail in Oregon and California. In the film, Reese Witherspoon makes the hike in an Oscar-nominated performance that finds her in almost every frame, fighting her way through

continued...

an idealistic, off-the-grid wilderness quest where the biggest threat still comes from bored dudes. Laura Dern co-stars as the adventurer's mother (earning an Oscar nomination for Best Supporting Actress), Everclear's Art Alexakis shows up as a tattoo artist, and Oregon's all over the screen, from Crater Lake and Mount Hood to the Oregon Badlands Wilderness and the Bridge of the Gods at Columbia River Gorge.

Conclusion

Beyond the couple hundred movies showcasing the Pacific Northwest as setting and subject, the region itself is a film lover's paradise, packed with film festivals, cherished movie houses, and inspired repertory events.

In Washington, you'll find the Seattle International Film Festival (SIFF), officially the biggest film festival in the United States, which fills nearly an entire month of late spring with new movies and ancillary events all over town. Beyond SIFF are nearly a dozen more festivals, which arrive in seasonal explosions. Spring brings the Seattle Asian American Film Festival, the trans-showcasing Translations Film Festival, and the Seattle Black Film Festival (hosted by the Langston Hughes Performing Arts Institute). Autumn brings Northwest Film Forum's Local Sightings fest (featuring new work by PNW filmmakers), the Seattle Queer Film Festival, the Tacoma Film Festival, the Port Townsend Film Festival, the Orcas Island Film Fest, and Tasveer, the largest South Asian film fest in the US.

As for non-festival delights, Seattle is home to top-tier repertory houses, including the crucial, artistically generative Northwest Film Forum, the brilliantly idiosyncratic Beacon Cinema, and the crowd-pleasing movie pub Central Cinema. If you're looking for something to please everyone, from little kids to high adults, head directly to Paramount Theatre's Silent Movie Mondays, where silent classics are regularly screened with live accompaniment from the Mighty Wurlitzer organ. If you're looking for something just for high adults, go to Collide-O-Scope, the mind-blowing montage extravaganza that hosts movie parties all over town, from the Fountain at Seattle Center to the Paramount.

Oregon is equally rich in film festivals. Winter brings the Portland International Film Festival, Oregon's biggest annual film event, founded in 1977 and produced by the Northwest Film Center. Spring brings Qdoc, the first-in-the-nation queer documentary film festival, as well as the Hollywood Theatre's Filmed by Bike fest, featuring bike-themed short films from around the world. Autumn brings a festival avalanche, with the POW Film Fest (aka the Portland Oregon Women's Film Festival), the Portland Film Festival, the Portland Queer Film Festival, and the Oregon Independent Film Festival.

Portland is also home to a shocking number of arthouse cinemas, including the camp-friendly cinema pub Cinemagic, the iconic arthouse Cinema 21, the old historic Hollywood Theatre, the even older and more historic Clinton Street Theater, the beloved second-run Academy Theater, and the ancient cinema-turned-movie pub the Laurelhurst. (And the 99W Drive-In shows double features for $9.)

Thematic Binge Lists

Under the banner of Pacific Northwest Cinema is a number of subgenres, each trafficking in distinct vibes and pleasures. If you're looking to explore a theme/sustain a mood, here's a handy guide.

PNW Romance
10 Things I Hate About You (page 5)
Benny & Joon (page 14)
Dogfight (page 29)
Laggies (page 45)
Late Autumn (page 50)
Life or Something Like It (page 50)
Love Happens (page 52)
An Officer and a Gentleman (page 54)
Overboard (page 123)
Safety Not Guaranteed (page 63)
Say Anything (page 65)
Singles (page 67)
Sleepless in Seattle (page 69)
Twilight (page 79)

PNW Creepfests
Brand Upon the Brain! (page 19)
Cthulhu (page 24)
Elephant (page 96)
The Ring (page 62)
The Road (page 10)
Twin Peaks: Fire Walk with Me (page 58)

Family-Friendly Flicks
Free Willy (page 105)
Harry and the Hendersons (page 41)
Kindergarten Cop (page 115)
The Goonies (page 108)
The Last Mimzy (page 49)
Short Circuit (page 134)

Acknowledgments

Thanks to those who took time to talk to me about PNW cinema, including filmmakers Megan Griffiths, Lacey Leavitt, and S. J. Chiro, and film writer and critic Kathy Fennessy (who I chatted up in hopes of getting a mention of the Seattle Film Critics Society in this book, and here it is). Additional thanks to Seattle's Scarecrow Video for stocking a bunch of PNW movies I wouldn't have been able to see otherwise, and personal thanks to the intense film-loving cultures of both Seattle and Portland, which make keeping fluent in arthouse cinema a beautiful communal pursuit.

Sources

The key resource for this book is the films themselves, which I
viewed through commercial streaming platforms, old-school
Netflix mailer DVDs, and Seattle's Scarecrow Video (with a couple
of the smaller, odder works found on YouTube and Vimeo). But
determining which movies to watch and perhaps include involved
consulting numerous existing roundups of movies made in Seattle
and Portland, which ranged from online listicles to print-media
overviews to museum exhibits. Among the consulted works:
Robert Horton's 2012 Museum of History and Industry exhibit
Celluloid Seattle: A City at the Movies; the database maintained
by the City of Seattle's Office of Film and Music; the websites
MovieMaps.org, HistoryLink.org, Decider.com, TheMovieDistrict.
com, TheCinemaholic.com, and WelcometoTwinPeaks.com;
archival reviews and profiles from *The International Examiner*,
Seattle Post-Intelligencer, *Willamette Week*, *Portland Monthly*,
and *Seattle Times*; Randy Hodgins and Steve McLellan's rollicking,
punchline-filled 1995 book *Seattle on Film: From the Jet City
to the Emerald City Through the Movies*; the Internet Movie
Database; and the Oregon Film Museum.

Index

About the Author

David Schmader is a writer devoted to exploring his obsessions, from homophobic rock stars and pray-away-the-gay Christians to trash cinema and legalized drugs. From 1998–2015, Schmader worked as a staff writer and editor for Seattle's Pulitzer-winning newsweekly *The Stranger*, writing film reviews, investigative essays, and the issue-opening column "Last Days: The Week in Review." In his spare time, he is the world's foremost authority on the glorious terribleness of the movie *Showgirls*, hosting annotated screenings of Paul Verhoeven's notorious stripper drama at cinemas all over North America and providing the commentary track for the *Showgirls* DVD. His first book *Weed: The User's Guide* was published by Sasquatch Books in 2016, with subsequent editions published in Denmark, Australia, and the United Kingdom.

About the Illustrator

Ashod Simonian is the coauthor of T*he Portland Book of Dates,* and author of *Real Fun,* a book of photography and stories documenting his decade spent touring the world in a variety of indie rock bands. He also cofounded the niche perfume brand Imaginary Authors and a nail polish company rooted in joy and activism called Claws Out.